Christian Politics

DONALD SOPER

Christian Politics

AN INTRODUCTION

London EPWORTH PRESS

7162 0287 5

Enquiries should be addressed to
The Methodist Publishing House
Wellington Road
Wimbledon
London SW19 8EU
Printed in Great Britain by
The Garden City Press Limited,
Letchworth, Hertfordshire SG6 1JS

Contents

1	Politics	7
2	Christianity and Politics	12
3	Compromise	20
4	Law and Order	29
5	Violence	40
6	Race	49
7	Poverty	59
8	Education	70
9	Liberty	81
10	Socialism	93

1 Politics

This small document is offered as a primer on the general subject of Christianity and politics; more precisely on the ethics of Christianity as derived from its theology, in relation to the ethics of politics similarly derived. But first a confession—and then a warning. The confession is as obvious as it is necessary: the task is very much too large for me adequately to deal with. It has proved over the centuries of the Christian era to be too much for very much greater minds than mine and the widespread avoidance of the theme by the spokesmen of the Church is evidence of the profound difficulties that emerge the moment Christianity and politics are looked at together. Nonetheless, I believe the theme to be unavoidable and I shall be satisfied if some of the guide-lines leading to a true resolution of the problem of Christian political ethics can be seen more clearly in what follows.

The warning is equally necessary, though not perhaps as obvious. I have learnt, after a long and sometimes painful experience, that the prerequisite of any effective enquiry on any topic is to make as sure as is possible that the words, and particularly the nouns, employed convey the writer's meaning with maximum precision.

Bearing these things in mind, I will endeavour to

say something about the meaning and characteristics of the word 'politics', to apply a similar process to the word 'Christianity', to examine the ethical relationship between the two and, finally, to consider how this relationship can come alive in specific areas of our affairs today.

To begin, then, with politics. It is an activity in thinking and doing, undertaken by human beings, and there is an all-important beginning here to the understanding of what is called human nature. Strictly speaking, it is impossible to define a human being; he can, at best, be described for, unlike things, human beings are open-ended and, inasmuch as politics is a human activity, the best we can do is to describe something of its nature and enumerate its salient characteristics. 'Politics', therefore, is the word we use, not to exhaust the meaning of man's behaviour patterns, but to specify certain of his ideas and actions and in particular those which concern the day by day business of living together with his fellows. This 'conduct' is economic in that it has to do with his physical needs: food, clothing and shelter and the ways in which these needs are met. It is social in that it is concerned with the law and order which are required to manage the various tensions that are inevitable in the 'get together' of the human species. In a short sentence: politics is the way things happen, or are caused to happen, to man as a social animal. If he were not gregarious, he could not be political; but, as he is much more than a pack animal, politics will not remain static like the social economy of—

shall we say—the beehive. The politics, so to speak, of the bee tends to remain uniform and unchanging, because this extraordinary creature appears to have achieved a stabilized society, and the dance of the workers at the portals of the hive have remained the same yesterday, today, and, as far as we know, for ever. But whatever else can be said about man, he possesses the means and the incentives of change; change in his environment and thereafter and, accompanying that change, change in his behaviour—and all this of course is reflected in his politics.

Politics then as an activity—a basic activity—may be an unchanging characteristic of the human species because it belongs to human nature, but the various expressions of that activity will always reflect man's changing patterns of behaviour. We are determined by our human nature; we are conditioned by our human behaviour. Human behaviour patterns can be influenced for good or evil by the creation of a good or evil climate and an environment which stimulates goodness or badness (I shall hope to treat of this in some detail later on) and this has always been the case. But unmistakably moral effects can now be achieved by genetic engineering, by all sorts of mechanical devices which have much more than merely mechanical effects. This is yet another characteristic of politics, which is the natural sequence of its extension and its competence. Politics has become increasingly ideological. Political ideals and actions have crystallized into systems of thought and codes of practice, some with prescribed limits, such as, for example, British Conservatism, others claiming final explanations and practices, such as Communism. But the increasing assumption is that the philosophy of politics is the queen of the sciences and political truth is all that man needs to resolve his problems and fulfil his destiny. Dialectical materialism is the most closely argued ideology which makes such claims and in one form or another the disciples of Marx and Engels are impressing this claim on a quarter of the world's population today.

Christianity is therefore confronted not only by other world faiths, with their credal and theological differences, but for the first time by a political development in which the area and competence of politics have vastly increased. The realm of politics has acquired most of the appurtenances of a world religion, with the universal application, inclusive authority and final applicability that are claimed for a universal faith. If then politics is the way things happen, and it would be foolhardy to deny the substance of such a claim, then is there not a head-on collision to be recognized with the Christian faith, which surely cannot be satisfied with a lesser claim? If politics is the way things happen, all kinds of things have been happening badly and the world of politics is infected with all sorts of social diseases, some of which increasingly look as if they are terminal. What is the key to the question of right and wrong and does organized Christianity provide that answer? In short, what is the relationship, if any, between Christianity and politics? Such are some of the inescapable questions which the Christian must face if he is to justify the central article of his faith, that Jesus not politics is the Way, the Truth and the Life.

2 Christianity and Politics

What then is this relationship of Christianity, and especially Christian ethics, to the modern Leviathan called politics? I will attempt the beginning of an answer now, and will endeavour later on to spell out the ethical principles of that Christian faith, as they are involved in such a relationship, under some of the headings of particular religio-political issues. Of course, if it could be shown that intrinsically no relationship exists between the two ways and means of life, then the enquiry is foreclosed; it should be remembered that such a complete separation has been frequently sponsored and vigorously argued from Scripture. The contention is that the Gospel carries an exclusively spiritual message, proclaiming the personal gift of its own life to those embracing its conditions and by faith and penitence enjoying a personal relationship with Jesus, the Saviour. In the interests of this preoccupation with the next world— for that is what it is—the all-important thing is to make a good death rather than work out a good life and, in the words of the hymn I was encouraged to sing in Sunday school, to remember that 'I am but a stranger here, Heaven is my Home'.

I will not delay to argue the case for or against such a view of Christianity, but it is important, if it is to be repudiated—and I am completely satisfied that it must be so repudiated—to recognize with sympathy how natural it was to invest the purely personal future as the Christian hope when it was well-nigh impossible to credit the present with its possibility or to conceive of it in any social context. As Bertrand Russell has rightly said, 'Up to the seventeenth century in the West, almost all thinking was about death'. However, the Gospel must stand or fall in terms of its relevance to the whole of life and, whatever we think of the past, we know that we live today in conditions of life on this planet with immeasurably greater opportunities of fulfilment than ever before. Unless Christianity relates to them, it has lost the greater part of its significance. I am sure that it does. Jesus spoke in the present tense and said that His Kingdom is here, within us and amongst us.

Strangely enough, the question of irrelevancy has again been used to defend the separation of political from spiritual ethics or drastically to curtail the relationship between them. According to the school of apocalyptic theologians, and apparent in the attitude advocated by the synoptic gospel writers, God's Kingdom was about to be dramatically and suddenly introduced by divine fiat, and therefore politics, at the time of our Lord, had but a very short term to run; consequently, all ethical contacts with the political world were strictly 'interim'. Now I find no evidence that Jesus subscribed to such a belief and am reinforced in that conviction as I read St John's Gospel, where it finds no room at all. In any case, it has not happened, and therefore we either admit that Christian ethics were for transitory occasions and no longer apply because they were based on historical miscalculations, or we hold fast to the teaching of Jesus as being fundamental and as pertinent to our generation as it was when He first proclaimed the Gospel. The very existence today of a Christian morality depends on the rejection of its limitation to a situation which, in fact, did not arise. Nevertheless, for practical as well as theological reasons, this conjunction of political and Christian morality has presented such formidable difficulties that, in various ways, evasive action has been repeatedly taken. The attempted unity, for example, of Church and State in the baptism of the Roman Empire as ecclesiastically holy and the investiture of the Catholic Church as secularly established produced in Christendom notable examples of morality such as 'just price' and the guild system in industry, but it never succeeded in marrying the Sermon on the Mount to the *Lex Romana*; the moral lines were parallel, at best, and broke down whenever a single track was attempted.

With the Reformation the emergent nation states abandoned the effort altogether, rejected the idea of a universally Christian ethic, at least in what is called the ultra-montanism of Rome, and substituted the Divine Right of their kings for the divine authority of their bishops. Yet the polarization of morality as either Christian or political was not fully accomplished until the rise of the economics of capitalism

14

within the emergent nation states. With all its failures and frustrations, priests and politicians did continue to hold that morality was indivisible, even if they could not make a go of it. Capitalism, as R. H. Tawney has shown, gave the *coup de grâce* to this forlorn hope. In practice, a true relationship between the two finally broke down because, in theory, they were mutually contradictory. Capitalism, even in its pre-industrial era, required, in order to secure its results, a framework of behaviour which was based on self-interest, enlightened or not; it had to find a code of morals of its own, because it could not derive them from the Gospel, let alone from the Cross. This it proceeded to do and, in doing it, abandoned both the Roman and the Christian moral code for an ethical system independent of everything except its usefulness in the promotion of its own ends. Marx and others have filled out Tawney's argument in their insistence that the law and the order of political, and indeed of cultural, institutions in our modern society, are built as a superstructure on the so-called ethics demanded by economics. In this respect I find the Marxists' case unanswerable, even if I find it overplayed at times and even if I find many of its remedies quite unacceptable.

This does not mean that all capitalists abandoned every vestige of the morality that comes from Galilee and from Golgotha. The private lives of Methodist capitalists, for example, in matters of teetotalism and personal chastity, cannot be impugned and often they sincerely believed that their care for the spiritual

15

welfare of their workers was sufficient to justify an indifference to the economic lot of the workers, a condition which they even claimed to be pre-ordained. What it has meant, and continues to mean, is that whatever lip-service is given to the need for the ethics of the Faith to be applied to the running of the State, so long as the ends of political action and those of Christianity are mutually hostile, there can be no accommodation.

Recently, attention has been invited by Christian thinkers and practitioners, who totally reject the notion that Christianity is not involved in politics, yet, at the same time, appreciate the almost overwhelming difficulty of a Christian-political answer to problems which come in the secular field, to what they call 'situational ethics'. The claim is, I am afraid, little more than a *cri de coeur*, based on genuine, sincere, but wishful thinking that the question will itself provide the answer, however urgent and complex that question is: 'sufficient unto the day', so to say. Just because Jesus did not formulate an ethical creed, I do not believe that His followers are exempt from so doing. In fact, His immediate followers in Acts, Chapter II, did precisely that and did it in his name. Is not this 'situational' proposition in principle like the old Apocalpyse idea coming back in a new form, and is it not as unacceptable? I am satisfied that it is.

To sum up this general enquiry about the challenge presented to politics by the moral claim inherent in Christianity, there appear to be three considerations

16

• •

which are peremptory and unchanging. First, the challenge is unavoidable, except at the price of denying the universality of Jesus and his Cross. If politics is the way things happen, then a Christianity which stands on the side-lines of that action is unworthy and irrelevant.

Secondly, the relationship between the two must be seen within a historical context. A Christian morality cannot finally be based on theological or metaphysical propositions which have nothing to do with time, like the Apocalyptic Vision. Seeing the Kingdom of God, like seeing the nation state, must be a perception within history as well as *sub specie aeternitatis*.

Thirdly, morality as a means is finally dependent on the ends to which that morality is directed. Political morality serves ever-widening areas with ever-increasing efficiency and even more explicit ends in view. Christian morality is inseparable from the Kingdom of God; its end is the Glory of God in his finished creation. These ends, at present, are radically separable from one another, wherefore the attempt which has been made to accommodate both moralities under one roof is foredoomed to failure. I shall presume to think that this summation is broadly true; in fact I believe it to be self-evident in the exact meaning of that phrase, and I will therefore accept the lesson which is to be drawn from it. If Christians are not prepared to see their religion as a series of pious noises in peculiar places, at one and the same time increasingly irrelevant, impotent, escapist and historically outdated, then they must seek the achieve-

17

ment of Christian morality, pre-eminently in the 'field of actuality'. The alternative was suddenly put the other day by a cynic who said that the omnipotence of God is no longer of interest to those who know the omnicompetence of politics. The burning question for the would-be Christian optimist is—how is that almighty power (a better phrase than the word omnipotence) to operate in the life of God's children? The equally ardent answer is—by changing the system, surely, which now frustrates that goodness and by creating the sort of social climate which would encourage it. So what follows will be an attempt to see that task against the backcloth of various issues, facing and, in most cases, threatening our modern society. I hope that the general strategy of the exercise will emerge in the course of the examination of the particular tactics that, for a Christian, each of these issues requires.

Finally, there remains the obligation to say something about the meaning and characteristics of Christianity. It need be only brief, for the rest of the book should disclose it more fully. I shall have occasion to refer to 'the teaching of Jesus' and 'the Sermon on the Mount' as a determinative part of Christianity. This does not imply a conviction that these are invariably the *ipsissima verba* of Jesus, for developments in New Testament scholarship have shown that such a contention cannot be sustained. It is however to accept that in the recorded words of Jesus, mediated to us through the New Testament writers, we possess a significant part of the meaning

18

and characteristics of Christianity. To them has to be added the further interpretations and expressions of the Gospel in the life of the Church as recorded in the New Testament. In all this Jesus is the central figure and 'the meaning and characteristics of Christianity' are to be found in him.

3 Compromise

If, as I have tried to show, the problem created by the inevitable confrontation between political and Christian claims is essentially one to be identified with the systems in which these claims are made, then it is sensible to begin the enquiry into the particular aspects of that problem by looking at the question of Church and State, for that is where historically it began, and that is where it still is.

The Kingdom of God, once it had to do with time as well as eternity—that is, once it had to be lived out and worked out in an earthly environment—found itself inescapably *vis-à-vis* a secular Kingdom: the Roman Empire and, for the early Christians, Judaism as well. The ensuing conflict, accommodation, detente, entente—and, from time to time, it was all of these—are stages in that saga in the story of Church and State; a story, by the way, not peculiar to the European West. Holy Russia is the somewhat contentious title of an almost identical confrontation in the Christian East, and the story of Turkey, to go further afield, is a similar tale of the relations of Islam, that heresy of the Christian Faith, with the temporal powers within which it tried to live and in which it flourished. The story, though possessing particular manifestations, is, I would think, invariably the same in the religions of the East. However, what is particularly significant for the present purpose is that this story offers prime evidence, not only of the characteristics of the process, but also of judgements which can be of practical use in the attempt today to resolve the competing claims of Church and State in a synthesis, which hitherto has proved unattainable.

To make a start, then, with these relations between what was called the Imperium of Rome and the Sacerdotium of the Church. There is the clearest example of the fundamental difficulty, the moment that relationship is viewed from the standpoint of morality. Politics, on the one hand, has been rightly described as the art of the possible and hence its morals are conditional and tentative and, in almost every case, the end will justify the means. For example, war, which I have already quoted Clauswitz as saying is a continuation of politics, is the most conspicuous example of this justification. Killing, enslaving, hating, lying are manifestly immoral in themselves, yet are politically acceptable in war and indeed in terrorism, when the so-called higher morality of the preservation of the State is at issue. Contrariwise, such immorality is equally justified in the field of terrorism, when it is enlisted to serve the interests and the revolutionary political objectives of those whose intention is to oppose the State. If indeed the nineteenth century developed and codified the theorem that war is an extension of politics, albeit using different means, it could surely be agreed that the twentieth century has done a similar job on the theorem that terrorism is a continuation of war,

21

though not so much by other means as by the inevitable explication of means already inherent in war.

Christianity, on the other hand, is the proclamation of the impossible: it is first the gift of God and only thereafter the accomplishment of his children. Therefore, Christian morality is much more a counsel of perfection than a code of ethics; or rather it is a counsel of perfection before it can ever be a code of ethics. Political morals by contrast are specific and practicable exactly because they are tailored in the first instance to the needs of the existing State; and it must be admitted, in the twentieth century, that no moral holds are barred. In this regard, there is a very powerful addition to this argument to be found in Dostoevsky's *Crime and Punishment* and *The Brothers Kamarazov*: it is what the French call *tout est permis*, 'everything is permissible'. With his incomparable psychological insight, Dostoevsky puts into the mouths of his characters the logical outcome of an ethical system which rejects the absolute authority of a God. Morality becomes totally subject to certain over-arching intentions and programmes. On the other hand, Christian morality has that absolute quality and therefore, in the first instance, it is an intention or an ideal rather than a programme or a practice. Why? Well, because it belongs to a realm which is yet to be, whereas politics is inseparable from things as they are.

There are of course exceptions to this general analysis and there are areas where political and Christian morals do coincide. I shall be arguing at

some length, in a subsequent chapter, that ι
a political system approximates to the natuι
Kingdom of God, the greater obviously is ι
gruity between the respective ethical requirem   ᴜ of
both. For example, the political morality of a genuine
Welfare State is much nearer the Christian morality
of loving one's neighbour, and consequently there is a
wider area of comparability than in the political
morality of, shall we say, a racist totalitarian regime.
It should be mentioned, moreover, that there are
ethical principles, such as those of personal chastity
and teetotalism within Christianity, comparable with
almsgiving in Islam, which are relatively independent
of the prevailing institutions, both ecclesiastical and
social. Even here, however the Marxists would argue,
as they do in the Communist Manifesto, that sexual
problems in a capitalist society, or sexual practices in
a capitalist society, are profoundly affected by the
prevailing modes of production, distribution and
exchange.

There is an important lesson here which, if learned,
goes a long way to explain the lack of realism in
much recent Christian foolhardy thinking, and it does
not need a modern Dostoevsky to expound it. The
emphasis that the Church has put on the social evils
like drink and gambling and personal sexual immorality is almost as much a confession of failure
as it is a matter of conscience. Let no one imagine
that I would defend any of them. As a would-be
member of the Kingdom of God, I am a teetotaller; as

a socialist, I oppose the capitalist practice of gambling; and, as a sacramentalist, I believe in chastity as opposed to sexual irresponsibility. The trouble starts when social and political concern to remove such evils takes the place of a more comprehensive social and political conscience about much greater and system-geared ends, like war and the economic system itself. In any case, drinking and gambling, like sexual aberrance, as Marx rightly argued, are intimately bound up with the economic systems in which they flourish and a concentration on the comparably uncomplicated ethics of personal behaviour becomes an escape hatch from the much more demanding and complex questions that lie behind them.

So, in short, whatever modifications in detail have to be made in the relationships between the moralities of Church and State, this one fact emerges, as pinpointing the difference between the two: political morality, with its inbuilt characteristic of relativity, that is its acknowledged subservience to political ends, and its preparedness to change or even abandon its canons of behaviour in the commanding interests of the State, is unashamedly casual and expedient. It is the secular counterpart, if you like, of situational ethics. Christian morality, on the other hand, as I have tried to argue, has an absolute quality about it, which as an ideal or objective is unchanging but, by that same token, is incapable of instant performance as it stands. For unlike the morality of the politician, which is geared to things as they are, the morality of the Gospel presupposes things which are not yet. So there is no alternative (and this is the nub of the matter) to compromise, if Christian morality is to be practical politics.

Now it should not be inferred from the foregoing that political morality necessarily represents practical politics. The single proposition of this chapter is that some element of compromise, both in the delineation and the carrying out of the ethics of the Sermon on the Mount, is absolutely inevitable, if that morality is to be more than an idle dream by an irrelevant Church. And, it must be added, the personal piety of members of the Church, despite all the sentimental evangelisms of this or any other day, is quite insufficient to turn such wishful thinking into the stuff of creative action. The road of private goodness is no way to the Kingdom of God, if it is a substitute for social morality. Involvement is inescapable, but the price to be paid is the acceptance of modifications of that morality, if the Christian ethic is not to prove totally inapplicable. This involves compromise. There is no other word that will do and, however regretfully we look at it, not to look at it will not persuade it to disappear, and denouncing it as unacceptable of course is hypocritical.

Let us, by all means, condemn that sort of compromise which Jesus himself condemned in the lives of some of the Scribes and Pharisees. Compromise with an obligation because it requires a self-denial which the would-be Christian is not prepared to make is as blameworthy now as it was in the first century. What is vitally important is to recognize that other

25

kind of compromise that is unavoidable if Christian morality is to get its foot in the political door. The problem bristles, of course, with difficulty and it should cause no surprise that the theology of compromise has been so greatly neglected hitherto. Everything in the contemporary situation renders such an informed theology more urgent than ever, and there is evidence of the way in which this ignored problem has, nevertheless, gnawed at the minds of honest Christian thinkers, and echoes of this limitation of ethics, as practised even by Jesus, has often been sounded in the realm of pure theology. Original sin is one of them, with its epidemic contamination; another is the claim made by some Christian thinkers, tortured by this problem, that Jesus took sin for our sakes. Such considerations belong to another document than this. It is the practical consideration within the light of modern political capability that demands attention and hitherto has received too little of it. I do not believe that there is an inclusive over-all answer, yet, if the destination of perfect goodness is beyond us, it is still possible to set out on the journey and, if we can catch the spirit of Jesus, we may have the wages of going on and getting increasingly nearer to his goal.

We already know that in intention we can embrace the Christian ethic in every sphere of human life. In our hearts and in our minds we can cherish the Kingdom of God as a personal realm of obedience and fellowship. Nothing need prevent us from also intending that Kingdom in the fields of politics and economics. In the Sermon on the Mount Jesus put such intention higher in the ethical code than actual performance. Again, there are areas of our life and environment where the Christian ethic can receive an immediate response. The liar can begin to tell the truth, not everywhere perhaps, but in vast areas where he now lies; the lecher can begin to be pure in heart and in whatever economic environment eschew the wickedness of irresponsible sexual indulgence; the unloving, even within a society which encourages self-interest and, in many cases, even discredits love, may in fact begin to care. As, however, these moral demands stretch into his social life, as he seeks to translate them from the language of personal faith and penitence and reliance on the power of prayer and the ministries of Christian fellowship into the language of Acts of Parliament and wages and the distribution of wealth and physical and mental security, he will still need penitence and faith and prayer and fellowship but—and it is a colossal but—he will need something more: the courage, the patience and the humility to recognize that, until the Kingdom of God comes, its moral attributes can only partially be applied to the existing political and economic kingdom. This is a fact of life. It is part, if you prefer it, of the grim mystery of sin and the evidence, as we must surely agree, of the almost overwhelming power of sin; almost because for the Christian to accept the fact that compromise is not the end of faith is, in so many of our human affairs, the beginning of the pilgrimage.

27

Now in the various economic political issues, which I will try to look at in the following chapters, I will endeavour to spell out again something of what, in the first place, the Christian ethic is and how we may begin, even with compromise, to express it today, and to move towards that uncompromising Christian ethic, in a political climate which not only makes it possible but will become its willing and complete servant.

4 Law and Order

To make any constructive attempt to consider Christian morality in that political area covered by the phrase 'Law and Order' requires special care. The phrase has acquired an aura almost of sanctity in some quarters, and is used to convey the proposition that the preservation of the *status quo* in political matters is of supreme importance and therefore the preservation of the law which authorizes that status and the order which guards it are equally sacrosanct. To quote St Paul, and I am afraid that this is what he meant, 'the powers that be are ordained of God' and so to subvert them is inevitably sinful.

If this is agreed, then law and order would constitute the first charge on any political system and rebellion would invariably be condemned. Such a view must be rejected, if only because social changes thereby would be automatically prohibited or, contrariwise, those who invest the maintenance of law and order with these absolute characteristics would be quite happy to use them both to make changes to their own advantage; and it is a recognizable fact that those who regard law and order as a kind of sacred cow are the first people to fulminate against any rejection of it by people on the other side of the political fence. However, 'law and order' has a genuine connotation, and to get to a workable description of the phrase, for the present discussion, it will probably suffice to say that any political system needs a structure of regulations and the organized means to protect them, and law and order answer those needs. As political systems have to do, however, with people, society must seek to make law and order enforceable on its members and hence it has, especially perhaps, to do with crime and punishment. This chapter will be concerned with the maintenance of laws rather than their rectitude; the question as to the rightness or wrongness of the laws themselves will find its place in a chapter on the constitution of the Kingdom of God. It is, in short, the political and Christian attitudes to crime with which we are here concerned and, initially, crime must be clearly distinguished from sin, although they are weeds from the same root. A sin becomes a crime when its performance is not only a personal act of disobedience of a moral principle, but when that performance also involves others, when in fact the wrongdoing of the individual has social consequences. This is a rough and ready distinction for, strictly speaking, there is no sin, not even the most private of vices, like sexual perversion, which can be entirely separated from social consequences. Nevertheless, there is a private sector in the realm of ethics and even the most totalitarian regimes do not pretend to legislate for everything from the cradle to the grave. How then ought society to react to those individuals by whose behaviour the welfare of society is threatened?

30

The political answer is in two parts. First, the effort must be made to prevent a possible crime, or to contain it; secondly, provision must be made for apprehending and dealing with the criminal. The preventive or anticipatory function is mainly undertaken by the officers of the law, although, as was evident in the last chapter, the final sanction still belongs to the armed forces of the realm. The arresting and punishing function is, in the first instance, also a police action; thereafter it becomes the duty of a court to prescribe a sentence, and then for society to see that such a sentence is carried out. This is done by police and others like them—for example, by probation officers—where the penalty is a fine or a condition of residence. On the other hand, it is imposed by prison authorities, where segregation is prescribed. There are variations, modifications and, recently, great and good changes in the overall pattern of punishments but, to consider what should be the moral judgement of Christians in relation to this chain of events, I shall endeavour to show that such a general moral judgement is not invalidated by the changes that have been taking place in various links in that chain.

As in all these matters a Christian judgement is the outcome of Christian approach. To begin with, the maintenance of law and order does require some use of force, and a police force is not incompatible with non-violence. In fact the difference between genuine police force and military force can be an excellent example of the real difference between force

31

and violence. The unlimited, arbitrary, destructive violence of the soldier is in strict contrast to the restricted, delegated and only marginally destructive force of the policeman. The army is judge, gaoler and jury in its own affairs, whereas a police force is confined to one or at most two of those offices. Above all, a police force is the servant in the household of justice, or it should be; indeed, unless there is already a house of justice, then there is no service for the policeman to render. An army, on the other hand, is master of its own activities and, since its actions are entirely directed towards the physical defeat of its enemies, no holds are barred, no moral principles that might hinder victory or produce defeat are tolerable. The pacifist position then is compatible with the police force and recognizes that the degree of force, safeguarded by the foregoing considerations, is a necessary element in the application of Christian gospel to human beings living in society. At the same time, a Christian ethic which eschews the weapons of mass violence must insist that a police force is not armed with them. But here, as everywhere else, there will be a degree of compromise on the border lines, so to say, between legitimate instruments of preventive force and the impermissible weapons which kill. Tear-gas and the water cannon may well belong to the first category. Having had some fifty years' experience of political demonstrations where feelings can run high, where alcohol adds to the tension and where there is the provocation to violence by inflamed passion and so on, I still remain persuaded that the

32

employment of such force as can incapacitate a demonstration by inducing violent sneezing or disperse a frenzied mob by hosepipe is not necessarily contrary to the Christian ethic.

It is in the other area in which law and order must operate that this ethic, I believe, is in clear contrast to political practice. The State's reaction to the criminal is largely governed by the ideas of deterrence, retribution and public safety when, having apprehended him and convicted him, it proceeds to punishment. That punishment varies from binding him over to the imposition of a fine and to the sequestration of his goods and amenities, to his imprisonment and hitherto, in extreme cases, to taking his life. I will not delay to argue the case against the capital punishment as an impermissible expression of law and order. Suffice it to say that the one justification for it, that it has a deterrent effect which is 'special', is quite fallacious. Capital punishment is not only morally degrading, it simply does not work.

The Christian ethic, however, which repudiates the death penalty in the light of its concept of human values, must also repudiate the entire philosophy of punishment as it is now conceived and practised. Once recognize that every human being is the brother or sister for whom Christ died, and even the worst of men possesses a value which forbids any right to treat him as a means to an end rather than an end, however admirable that end may appear to be. Hence the only sort of punishment which can claim Christian approval is that in which the attempted reformation of the criminal takes precedence over everything else, even the welfare of the State. This may appear a hard saying and yet the Christian must insist that social security is not best safeguarded by programmes of revenge or making the punishment fit the crime or putting the criminal out of possible circulation. It is only when the punishment fits the criminal that the operation of law and order is acceptable in Christian terms. The kind of punishment that falls under the general category of the fine may qualify as being morally acceptable. However, in so far as it tends to reflect a capitalist economy it is likely to be unfair because the economic aspect of this sort of punishment which involves a statutory amount of fine will obviously fall more heavily on the poor than the more wealthy. The fine is also suspect because the person fined may well be able to raise by subscription among his friends and/or his unconvicted accomplices much or all of the cash required by the sentence. If this happens, then the genuine impact of the punishment will not fall upon the delinquent and the justice of this sentence will be subverted.

It is however what is called the 'prison syndrome' which still characterizes the attitude of the State to its offenders and which in principle is irreconcilable, as I would claim, with Christian morality. The philosophy of the prison system is historically simple to describe. This is how the traditional reaction to the evildoer goes: the criminal is a threat to general tranquillity or to the maintenance of a certain mode of life. therefore society must be innoculated against his

infection, so put him away and then his future de-
predations can be prevented and society can forget
about him. The prison system is a piece of social
cowardice masquerading as a piece of civilized conduct. Reform, of course, has made vast improvements
in recent years to the conditions of the prison system
and the intentions of those who administer it. Re-
duced sentences, parole measures, open prisons are
examples and I, like any other prison chaplain, can
testify to their benefactions. But the principle behind
the prison system remains and it is basically an un-
christian one. It is evasive, cowardly, unreformative
and, above all, it fails to do the one thing that lies at
the heart of the Christian gospel—to generate
penitence and to encourage faith and so to recover
the sinner. The short sentence is morally irrelevant
and in practice has no therapeutic value whatsoever.
What nonsense it is regularly to shut up the persistent
drunk for periods of fourteen days! The long
sentence, anything over six years in identical conditions of imprisonment, all too frequently damages
beyond recovery dimensions of hope and moral
ambition, which wither in the deadening routine of
prison life. The man who emerges from a long-term
penal sentence has been in most cases permanently
conditioned against recovery in the real world from
which so long he has been separated. I venture to
doubt, after years of experience of contact with
prisoners, whether any man is better because he has
been put in prison, though some have recovered
despite it. The Christian then should set his face

against the entire concept and apparatus of prison; but it is not enough to condemn, neither is it enough, as I would argue, to make the best of a bad job as a great deal of Christian advocacy and experiment in the field of prison reform has sought to do and has, in a measure, succeeded in doing.

Law and order, if they are to be true guardians of the good society, must repudiate the basic notion that underlies the policy of putting away and shutting up the anti-social members of that society. If such procedures, whereby criminals must be taken out of society in particular cases, are necessary—those, for example, involving the mentally deranged and the suicidal—custodial provisions must be regarded as a means of treatment and not as an end in themselves. It would be frivolous to claim that those who are mentally and morally sick and are a menace to others, especially when that sickness is characterized by symptoms that are sexually violent, should not be segregated until their condition is no longer infective.

No one in his senses would object to the segregation of someone suffering from a 'notifiable' disease such as typhus or yellow monkey fever, but of course there is a difference which must not be ignored. No blame whatsoever can be attached to the innocent victim of a virus infection. On the other hand, though there must be a degree of diminished moral responsibility in the case of the sex pervert or the homicidal criminal, it is the sheerest sentimentalism to regard him as totally without some measure of blame. Therefore, although treatment in the one case does not carry with it any element of penitence, recovery in the other case must do so. Then again, punishment should be lived out in the world and not away from it, and this means the imposition of restrictions, the application of required duties and intermittent custody, in many instances, of the actual person of the criminal.

Examples can help to clarify these modes of action in the entire structure of punishment but they should all of them be directed towards reform as their justification. The anti-social drunkard should be required to reside in a hostel, or in a bed-sit, where he will be encouraged towards sobriety, and subjected to such discipline as will show him that he is much more a patient in a convalescent home than a rascal in a prison punishment block. For those guilty of actions which are anti-social, in that they cheat their fellows out of their goods and amenities, there should be set up, instead of places of permanent imprisonment, semi-custodial institutions in which they would suffer a necessary degree of segregation, but also be required to make restitution in work and money to the society which has been impoverished by their previous behaviour. The further a wrongdoer can be removed from the effect of his wrongdoing on the people he victimizes, the more easily he can practise his wickedness. The nearer he can be brought to the personal effects of what he does, the greater the chance of remorse and of contrition. To establish a personal relationship in any human activity is the catalyst of reality and, if that sounds as if it comes from some learned tome on psychology, so it does. James Ward wrote it a century ago. There is an illustration from the arena of war which for me confirms it. If the airman dropping his bombs on an open city were compelled to go down with his napalm bomb and witness its horrible impact on just one child, he would be much less inclined, to put it mildly, to drop that bomb than when at twenty-five thousand feet he bombs an objective and sees nothing more than an orange burst and a cloud of smoke. Yet the only difference between putting a baby on the fire and putting fire on the baby is the remoteness of twenty-five thousand feet. By far the best chance of reformation is the establishment of a genuine relationship by which crime is seen and restitution is possible in personal terms. Where it has been tried in the field of punishment, it has been conspicuously successful as the Howard League knows and can present the evidence. Finally, and if possible, that restitution should be made to the individuals or groups of individuals who have suffered by their crimes. The all-important element in this kind of sentence is that the criminal should *remain* in vital contact with the very personalized world in which his reformed life must be lived out, the very world in which the present prison system regime makes him less capable of redeeming his past.

There is much more to be said and done. I have neither the competence to say it, nor the space to include it. There is much informative literature for those prepared to read it coming out of Communist countries alongside the less worthy practices which have received such widespread publicity and justly so. But, most important of all, the field of law and order exemplifies yet another aspect of the relationship of Christianity to politics. Just as the consideration of Church and State reveals, among other things, inevitable conflict, and the consideration of violence brings to light, among other matters, the fact of compromise, so an examination of the provisions necessary to protect a genuine programme of law and order opens up, for politicians and churchmen alike, the prospect of revolutionary change. It is not an excuse for the sketchiness of the nature of that change, as set down in this chapter, to be reminded of the pragmatic nature of Christian ethics and how fundamental is the dictum that he who doeth the will, shall know of the Gospel. That is an enabling truth. A great many of the problems involved in a change-over from a pagan prison system to a Christian reformative system, and a largely non-custodial one at that, will only become clear, let alone be solved, as we go along with them.

5 Violence

The wit who said, 'Nuclear energy is here to stay—
the important question is are we?' was calling attention to the issue of humanity which, in itself, dwarfs
all others, both in its magnitude and in its menace.
In its size, because our command of power, now
in the nuclear field, has vastly increased; in its menace,
because such power has been turned into actual
potential violence of an unprecedented kind—and
nuclear power in particular. And as has been already
said in these pages, politics enjoys that power and
exercises that violence. Where mass violence prevails
as it does, the question of violence itself is crucial to
any enquiry in which survival, let alone morality, is
under consideration. The possible field of direct action
to implement the Christian morality of the future,
which I insist must be pacifist, is however enlarged and
cultivable today, because of the development of mass
violence, with its lethal capacity, capability and above
all the impossibility of calculating its effects. Vietnam
and Northern Ireland, in particular, are lurid illustrations and grim warnings of not only the invalidity or
the immorality of the killings and maimings but, just
as much, of their futility. In both the secular and
spiritual areas, war as a continuation of policies—
good or bad—is profoundly untrustworthy as well
as morally dangerous.

What then is Christian morality in this field, and to what an extent is it capable of practical application? In fact, what can we do in the name of the Lord?

I think it would be churlish to deny to politics any moral ambitions or practices in this ominous situation. Briefly, the aim of politics except in extreme instances, such as, I suppose, the programme of the Borneo headhunters, is peaceful or, at least, is concerned with the reduction of violence. Those who oppose the regimes that owe allegiance to one or other of the revolutionary programmes associated with Marxist ideas are not entitled to deny to such regimes the intention of peace as a final objective. In fairness to them, they accept and practise violence as a necessary prelude to that eventual condition where war shall no longer be required. Here is an acute example of the claim that the end justifies the means, whereas the Christian must surely believe that the means will determine the end since, as has been written elsewhere in these pages, those who take the sword (for whatever end) will perish by the sword. It would, I imagine, be more difficult to define the Fascist or Nazi or Falangist doctrines in similar terms. The worst elements in these discreditable regimes are the assumptions that war is not only a means to an end, but an essential activity for a virile and progressive human society. The fact remains that as a general rule the State does entitle itself to the use of violence as a means to that end. Physical violence is countenanced in the interests of law and

41

order and practised by the officers of law, while mass violence, that is war, is accepted as the final bastion of the State and is regarded as the duty of its members in the last resort, when the State itself is threatened. So the State not only legitimizes violence but invests it under particular circumstances with ethical merit. This has been as true, and still is true, of primitive communities, as it continues to be true in sophisticated states in the present day. Most informed commentators would add that what we call civilization in the twentieth century is intrinsically more violent than at any period in the professed ascent of man. No one can deny that the means at its disposal now present, as I have said already, a terminal threat to our continued existence on this planet.

The chain reaction promoted by modern bombs is terrifying to contemplate—and this is not the prognosis merely of those who believe that there is a wrath to come and invite their fellows to flee from it; it is the sober, yet terrible conviction of scientists, who are in touch with the realities of nuclear power.

To look at violence now from the Christian standpoint indicates an initial similarity to the approach of the politicians; both, with exceptions such as have already been mentioned, condemn violence for its own sake and both feel able to do so because of an underlying optimism which is common to both. The similarity goes even deeper. Organized Christianity in the interest of the soul has sponsored physical violence, just as organized politics has enlisted it in the interests of law and order. The rack and the stake, however detestable they appear now, have been powerfully defended by the Church as justified in the permanent interests of man's eternal soul, and indeed, capital punishment is still widely defended as a justifiable deterrent to murder.

At the level of mass violence, the official position of the majority of Christian churches is that some wars may be regarded as just, though it is only fair to add that almost all the conditions that entitled a war to be so regarded in the past no longer exist. In the place of war as a set piece, urban warfare and guerrilla fighting now present the age-long problem of sanctifying violence in a new but equally agonizing form. Nonetheless most Christian organizations would still defend mass violence even of this nature as a justifiable last-ditch recourse in the absence, as they would claim, of any other means of social redress. Is there then a basic clash in this matter between political and Christian morality? I believe there is and, what is more, I am quite sure that practically everybody thinks that there ought to be. The contrast appears to me to be immediate and unmistakable: especially from the study of the Gospels and the practice of the Apostolic Church. Jesus proclaimed a non-violent overcoming of evil, and his Cross is not only the symbol of suffering love but also the instrument of our salvation from violence. Jesus's injunction to love one's enemy, to turn the other cheek to the assailant, who is making an insulting gesture as well as being physically aggressive, and his own example of this technique of pacifist reaction

43

to the violence of others contains no support for the suggestion that the way of the Cross must give place, under certain circumstances, to other practices in which violence will be required. The episode of the two swords or the occasion in the Temple of the turning out of the money changers—like other occasions in the public ministry where the words of Jesus and his actions give some substance to the assertion that the pacifist cause is insufficient in certain conditions—must be seen in the clear light of what Jesus himself did when the time came to practise, or to forsake, this way of non-violent resistance to evil which he declared in his teaching. The perfect correspondence between the words of Jesus, as he meant them to be understood, and his actions when he was required to put them into effect is the supreme example of practising what you preach, and the failure to appreciate this unity of thought and action in the historic Jesus is still one of the biggest stumbling blocks to Christian understanding, let alone discipleship. If I do not pursue this topic here, let me recommend John Ferguson's *The Politics of Love* (James Clarke and the Fellowship of Reconciliation) for a comprehensive and meticulous treatment of this particular proposition.

If Christian morality is pre-eminently obedience to Jesus, as the Way and the Truth and the Life, then is not the practice of violence under any conditions an act of disobedience in the clear light of this perfect example? Having made such a claim, however, it is in this realm that the acceptance of it is seen in its most acute and complicated and bewildering form. Are we not so mixed up in a world of violence that to avoid any contact with it is quite unrealistic? What are we to say when we think of Bonhoeffer and the cruel dilemma that the monstrous evil of Hitlerism presented to him as a theologian and at the same time as a citizen? Is not the guerrilla warfare undertaken by an oppressed people sometimes the only remedy for a social disease which remains impervious to any other available remedy? The choice for the Christian is indeed an unenviable one, because practical compromise must be part of a practical solution of the dilemma while conditions of mass violence prevail.

Christian perfection then is not on the cards and who knows it better than one who endeavoured to be a pacifist in wartime, when even to practise non-violence required the acceptance of an environment dominated by the war effort? In fact the only available programme that avoids the cowardice of a complete withdrawal from the battlefield is to make a minimum contribution to the violent process in order to make a maximum contribution to those other processes of comforting and loving and healing, and maybe of suffering, which will constitute the only final victory. The inclusion in this process of civil defence, chaplaincy, ambulance work, the payment of taxes and many other compromised issues can, I humbly believe, be part of the endeavour to obey the law of love in the midst of corporate violence. The choice or refusal of such compromises cannot be a matter of ecclesiastical decree, even by a Church

45

committed to pacifism, but it remains a necessary part of that pacifism. The overriding obligation is to retain in wartime a positive rather than a negative posture. The Christian pacifist may be unduly inhibited in the practice of non-violent love but he is not totally prohibited from pursuing it. He must accept the measure of compromise which a society at war imposes but he can and must be a pacifist and not just a passivist.

The foregoing, however, leaves the major question still unanswered: if Christianity is a revolutionary creed with a revolutionary ethic, then that ethic is capable of immediate application in situations which are ripe for sudden change. Politics recognizes that many of its intended changes must be evolutionary—that is, they must go hand in hand with developing circumstances. But alongside such Fabian gradualness, there are other conditions which constitute the appointed time for dramatic revolutionary changes. One of the clearest examples in modern times of such readiness for revolution was the Communist revolution under Lenin, but other examples can be found on many pages of the history book. Some of them are climatic like the fundamental conditions that from time to time produce ice ages or empty the granary of the Roman Empire to begin to become the Sahara of our day; some of them are circumstantial, like the European discovery of a New World across the Atlantic. Most of them are created by the conjunction in time of the operation of individual personalities and particular economic and social conditions, and here the distinction has to be drawn between what is evolutionary, even in such revolutionary situations, and what can happen more dramatically. Christianity has to be similarly interpreted. The good news to the poor—for example, the feeding of the hungry—must be in large part evolutionary programmes because the practical demands for the fulfilment involve a time lag, which in its turn involves a compromised programme at any particular time. Jesus, however, believed that peace-making was a revolutionary programme, because those who took the sword, even in his day, were to perish by it, and that non-violence was to be accepted immediately. Commentators have rightly stressed that such pacifism was not accompanied by a finished technique of social behaviour to take the place of the violent society of the Roman Empire. Nonetheless, Jesus believed that such a revolutionary commitment was 'sufficient unto the day' and that obedience on that particular day to its non-violent requirements would itself provide opportunities and possible actions in the future, which were not and could not immediately or even reasonably be apparent at the time.

It is this consideration which has persuaded me to embrace a pacifism which means a personal renunciation of war and a refusal to support any political expressions of violence, from capital punishment to participation in war. It obliges me to try to win Christians to declare themselves in similar fashion. The areas of compromise, in certain fields of violence such as, for example, violence to the animal creation,

47

must in some measure be temporarily accepted, though closely scrutinized; they must not become the excuse for not obeying the Christian ethic demonstrated by Jesus in his Way of the Cross. Further the inability to foresee the immediate results of such non-violent attitudes by Christians, acting individually and in concert, is no reason in the critical revolutionary situation that violence has assumed in our day for refusing to take the first step in obedience to the Christian ethic. That first step will allow tomorrow to take peaceful care of itself.

6 Race

The moral problems created by race today are of such complexity and magnitude that they cannot possibly be omitted from a discussion like this. It may well be that to find the true resolution in this field is about the most important of all the tasks facing politicians and Christians alike, yet there is a distinction to be drawn between issues like Church and State, Violence, Law and Order and those which centre upon race and express themselves today in various forms of racialism. In primitive society, for example, the first three are indigenous; they may vary in their scope and in their form, but they are in-built in essence. Race, on the other hand, has only to be taken into practical account under particular circumstances. For instance, where members of differing races for geographical and economic reasons were not in touch with one another, as happened in China for centuries, any idea of relationships between races was purely academic and, of course, no actual problem. However, racial groups thus segregated were not immune from the technological and scientific progress in the fields of communication, described earlier in these pages, and the story of the East India Company is a conspicuous illustration of what happens when members of different races can meet and get at one another; race becomes racialism, in ever-increasing degree, as the

49

world diminishes in size and as the give and take between hitherto separated human beings becomes possible.

It has so happened that the technological advance of the western world, whereby it has been able to exploit the opportunities of contact with what we now call the Third World, has produced political and economic results which make the racial issue today of paramount importance. In broad outline, the accident of western civilization, being the first to be able to lay hold of scientific power in its modern categories, has meant a particular world distribution or maldistribution of wealth whereby the Caucasian peoples are, generally, well off and the oriental peoples badly off. Worse still, it has meant that the white races from the West have baptized their power with the impudent assumption that it justifies them in believing that the brown and black and red people belong to an inferior breed and thereby are ordained (yes, 'ordained' is the word, as in the cruder concepts of apartheid) to be the hewers of wood and the drawers of water on behalf of their masters. And where there has been stimulation of industrial growth in the hitherto depressed areas of the Third World, that stimulation has not been primarily for the benefit of the inhabitants of these previously unfortunate areas, but for the further enrichment of their exploiters.

These facts have been cemented into systems, such as political imperialism and economic colonialization, the scramble for Africa and the slave trade. They are all episodes or elements in the history book of which

the contemporary reprints and re-editions are characterized by immigration, apartheid, eindrag and
population explosion. These are samples of changes
in attitude and culture now possible because the once
exploited world can flex muscles which, hitherto, only
their oppressors could develop. This record is not,
therefore, all bad and incidentally the white races have
bestowed many benefits on their now more or less
developed black and brown kinsmen. For example,
all the leaders of right and left in Ceylon were mis-
sionary educated and I wonder how many of the black
leaders in Southern Africa would have been active
today to advocate this repudiation of so much that
comes from Europe if they had not, as children,
received the medical and educational facilities offered
by the European missionaries and social workers.
Granted that the white invaders of India were carried
to financial profit on the backs of their Hindu servants,
those backs were incidentally strengthened in the
process. Such reflections as these are necessary. They
do not exonerate the exploiter but they do condition
his exploitation. The racialism that has become so vital
a factor in the modern set-up is mixed up with other
political, economic, structural and spiritual activities,
so that the broad outlines of the indictment should
not be regarded as a fully painted picture, as if race
can be isolated from the complex of social and
economic development. Of course it cannot. Moreover,
racialist practice is no longer confined to the unjust
treatment of black by whites. The evil lesson has, in
some cases, all too efficiently been learned by the black

peoples themselves and the African continent now unfortunately offers deplorable evidence of racialist policies in reverse. If there is white racialism in one place, there is black racialism next door.

Enough then has perhaps been said in this chapter to designate the nature of the problem of race, that is, its use for purposes of oppression or exploitation or discrimination, so that it has become a basic ingredient in political problems and so has imposed a basic responsibility upon the Christian to pronounce upon it. This he must do but with understanding, and with significance.

Historically, the beginnings of Christianity were not affected by racial questions in the exact sense of the word 'race' and many experts in this field would limit the word 'race' much more narrowly than is generally understood. On the other hand, relationships between Jews and Samaritans, Romans and Greeks, both predominantly political, cultural and religious, were already in apostolic times affected by the nature of the Greek and Roman imperialism, and to that extent, they were multi-racial issues. At the same time, what emphases on race resulted from an ecclesiastical source were largely subsumed under two heads: the theological concept of a chosen race, its privileges and responsibilities, and the peculiarly cosmopolitan nature of society in that part of the world in which Christian institutions began to take root. The attitude of Jesus, in so far as it affected racial questions, was therefore expressed within both a theological framework and the social divisions of his own time. It is idle to look for precise guidance from the Gospels or the early Church as to the sophisticated problems of immigration and discrimination and other racial matters which have more recent growth. What we can expect to find here, as in other fields, is a basis of moral principle, which was couched in first-century terms, but is equally applicable today. Jesus gave every evidence that he conceived his ministry as the fulfilment of God's purposes as they had been revealed to the Jewish people. He said that he was come to fulfil the law not to overthrow it, and that law represented the unique vocation of the race to which he belonged. For Jesus that fulfilment meant the extension far beyond his own race of all the promises and prospects of which they had been the custodians. The Gospel was to include all men everywhere, so for his followers the Kingdom of God is that global society in which we are all invited to practise brotherhood, because we can all say with assurance 'Our Father, Thy Kingdom come'.

In one of his most memorable sentences, St Paul catches the truth of this fundamental moral principle. Having described the changes that the Gospel can bring about in human lives he goes on to say: 'Here there cannot be Greek and Jew, circumcised and uncircumcised, barbarian, Scythian, slave, free man' (Col. 3:11). For an aristocratic Hebrew, equally proud of his Roman citizenship, here is first-rate evidence of the universality of the Gospel and its unmistakable implications wherever it was proclaimed.

Discrimination then on the basis of race is

absolutely incompatible with Christian morality but,
if we are to turn to the translation of this text, to the
concrete propositions, two thousand years after it was
first announced by Jesus, the problem for today can
appear all the more bewildering because, paradoxically
enough, the Palestine of two thousand years ago provided a cosmopolitan environment in which racial
tensions were comparatively few. The reason was an
economic one. Within the Roman Empire, the Middle
East (as we now call it) was one of the most important
crossroads of trade routes linking the widespread
Roman communities from east to west and also, sub-
stantially, from north to south. To use the Marxist
terms, and here they are clearly applicable, the
economic basis to life in such circumstances was
responsible for the superstructure of social attitudes.
A common language for this High Street was necessary and common Greek provided such a *lingua
franca*; the very class society made the idea of a
raceless society largely irrelevant; the economic difference was between master and servant, buyer and
seller, and in such a market economy the colour of a
man's skin was relatively unimportant. The caravan-
serai, whatever else it was, was multi-racial. For this
reason, Jesus could tell a story about a Samaritan
going down from Jerusalem to Jericho—a journey
which from a religious standpoint would have been
unthinkable and mortally dangerous, considering the
racial hostility bteween Jew and Samaritan. The pearl,
however, in the story was not racial but economic.
The Samaritan was not attacked by religious zealots

but by secular thieves. The Christian philosophy of race is unmistakable in the New Testament, the application of it cannot be separated from the historical process. The apostolic era was transitional, in both senses of the word, as has now been said many times in these pages, but it is so central to the argument that it deserves further emphasis. Racial questions today are not only the residuary legatees of more primitive societies; they are the outworkings of new social complexes, different in kind as well as in degree from their antecedents.

To try to deal then with immigration, apartheid and all the immediate problems of a multi-racial world is mandatory for the Christian but requires a degree of attention and a detail of answer impossible to achieve in a chapter or even in a volume. At best, some guidelines may be indicated. Most of them lie in anticipation and consideration of the constitution of the Kingdom of God—as far as it can be put into political and economic terms—and this will be attempted later on. Meanwhile there can and must be measures which should be immediately taken to enable Christian morality to get a toe-hold on the pathway to the destruction of racialism, and here I would offer some of them, albeit tentatively, because final elimination of the problems of race must await the sort of society in which alone the final victory may be won.

Whatever the cost to white or black prestige or to material advantage, Christians must demand equal educational, cultural and political opportunities for

55

those to whom they have hitherto been denied. For example, the Bantu education Act in South Africa cannot stand, neither can a wage system employed by entrenched big business in which the black worker receives only a tithe of the remuneration available to his white co-worker. Thus equality of opportunity is the only practical expression in social terms of· the Christian injunction to love your neighbour as yourself, and Jesus specified the neighbour as your fellow man, particularly when he is in a worse condition than you are. The Good Samaritan was that man in the parable and, so long as the independent nation-state persists, it will be the duty of its administration to seek the general welfare of all those who are within the borders of that state; and among other things, this will involve questions of population saturation, of the economic viability of its work force, its G.N.P. and the optimum number of its citizens. These questions are naturally affected by the migration and immigration that mobility makes possible. Those same administrators of the modern state must legislate in order to control such consequential variations in density of population and their attendant difficulties. This is mixed up with all sorts of problems such as national pride and the white man's burden. Just as important, it involves psychological tensions between psychologically different cultures, such as, for example, reaction to the smell of curry. Not least in this field are the ridiculous theories of racial purity, like those proclaimed by Dr Goebbels, who was, by the way, the physical contradiction of his own main thesis about the blond German. Worst of all, support is found for policies of apartheid in particular by treating holy writ as the reservoir of texts to be tapped in the service of programmes already agreed for other than holy reasons. South Africa and the Dutch Reformed Church are lamentable examples of this perversity although they are modern editions of exegetical perversities for which most Christian communities have reason to be ashamed. The Christian answer in these complicated fields, created by multi-racial modern states, is that an unregulated influx or efflux of people, especially of different races, cultures and conditions, in and out of a particular state is very often a piece of escapism. This is particularly so in the matter of immigration. Personal responsibility, moral responsibility, must be enforced to prevent a state of affairs where, with an unpredictable population, a predictable social policy is inhibited. This again is a compromise, or contains a compromise; it is an interim ethic promoted by the immense differences in living standards and living opportunities between states. Only when all men black, white, yellow or brown in all their separate conditions become the responsibility of all men, and the living standards of the countries from which men emigrate are lifted to the living standards of the lands to which they emigrate, will the brotherhood of man take the place of discriminations of race. Meanwhile Christians must press for political democracy in multi-racial society; for one man one vote, irrespective of colour, is the only basis of government which safeguards the supreme Christian principle of the dignity and infinite significance of the human being, wherever he comes from. Even if such majority rule is accompanied by growing pains, men like Kaunda and Nyerere, both professing Christians, are living testimonies to its practicability, whatever the differences of opinion as to certain elements in their administrations. Here again, he that doeth the will shall know of the Gospel. The beginning of the doing of that will may be imperfect and may be partial, but it is the inevitable first step.

7 Poverty

A visitor from outer space capable of making his impressions of this planet intelligible to us would probably mention, almost in his first sentence, something that we tend to lose sight of in our minds, because its very familiarity tends to breed a contempt for its significance. What is it? That if a minority of human beings have enough to eat and wear and somewhere to live, the great majority lack food and clothing and shelter, at least in such quality and quantity as to give a reasonable expectation of contentment, let alone happiness. The outstanding characteristic about human life is its endemic destitution. Most people in the world are physically and mentally impoverished. They are stunted in growth and enfeebled in health, because the basic necessaries of life are either not available or are chronically insufficient. They are also stunted, of course, in mental growth and enfeebled in mental health because the proteins and carbohydrates necessary for the informed mind are out of their reach. Their lives are nasty most of the time, brutish through no fault of their own and almost invariably short.

I hope the gentle reader will not be diverted from these generalizations either by reflecting on the undoubted improvements in the state of affairs that have taken place in the industrial revolution in the West, or by any of the literary nonsense perpetuated by Wordsworth and Coleridge about 'the noble savage'. Least of all will he be misled by the Marxist fatuity about primitive communism. The spiritual truths in the myth of the Garden of Eden are completely absent from this artificially constructed beginning of dialectical materialism. There was no golden classless primitive age. Human life began in poverty and despite all the changes, evolutionary and revolutionary, poverty at home and abroad is still the common lot, and to add insult to injury the gap between the 'haves' and the 'have-nots' is widening, not contracting. The rich are still getting richer much faster than the poor are getting less poor. In absolute terms, it is probably accurate to say quite bleakly that the one group is still getting better off while the other is getting worse off.

Now to leave these questions of comparative poverty, the question remains, what to do about the poor, and it is central to the business of all civilized governments. It cannot be ignored even by tyrannical ones. For this reason it has always appeared to me escapist, if not perverse, to ignore the quite basic economic question just because its most radical expression has come from the Marxists. So often the determination to oppose communism because of its manifest errors causes its opponents to ignore its equally manifest truths.

Reference has been made to the fundamental nature of the economic factor in preceding chapters, because it has been impossible to exclude it. In con-

siderations of race, violence or the state it is unavoidable. In these concluding chapters the economic
question will be treated as a foundation and not just
one floor, as it were, in the social building. I will
attempt to use the Marxist critique or rather those
elements in that critique which are shared by many
of its predecessors and which, I believe, are required
for any attempt to deal with the poverty with which
this chapter is especially concerned.

As a *servant* of constructive thinking, I believe
that Marxist critique to be invaluable; though, as a
master, I would find it intolerable. Marx, like so
many other prophets, was right in what he said and
often wrong in what he left out. He said, as I tried to
indicate earlier, that the prevailing conditions in any
society, which govern the way in which man gets his
basic necessaries, or does not get them, are the key to
his social state and to understand these economic
factors is to begin at the right place. Marx, or Marx
through the eyes of Engels, went much further. But
in these pages I have argued that whether man is
determined by his economic environment or only, as
I believe, conditioned by that environment, with
other elements in it beside the economic ones, the
significance of the economic factor remains imperative. The important thing is to accept the fact that
we are very largely the product of our environment
and in that environment the economic factor is pre-
dominant. There is nothing unworthy, let alone
impious, in Christians accepting this argument and
considering the morally right response that, in the

light of it, should be made to the issue of poverty in particular. The Christian is entitled to look for this kind of approach to economic questions in the Gospel, and sure enough he will find it. Here is some of the evidence.

Jesus began his public ministry, according to Luke, by taking up the plight of the poor, and by announcing that the fulfilment of the prophetic Good News, which was at the heart of the Hebrew prophets and their tradition, and was now imminent. 'Today', he said, 'hath this Scripture been fulfilled in your ears.' The first Beatitude was the proclamation of happiness for the poor and I think in this regard the French word *heureux* is nearer the original than the word 'blessed'; as the Negro preacher said, 'Happiness is not pie in the sky but ham where we am'. Jesus fed the five thousand not because they were good but because they were hungry, and to this practical philanthrophy he added a Christian economic philosophy which the Church, preoccupied with spirituality, has so often ignored. We should not be ashamed to thank Marx for reminding us, as I have suggested, of what that philosophy is.

The fundamentals are there for all to read in the Sermon on the Mount. As Jesus said, the way we should act to one another in the matter of food, clothing and shelter should reflect the providence of God. Man has an inalienable right to the means of life and that right has nothing to do with his moral condition.

Said Jesus, 'God sends His rain on the just and

the unjust'; he does not water only the good man's garden; the sun shines on the evil and the good; the birds of the air are economically shiftless and certainly ignore the prudent process of gathering into barns, but they are fed; the lilies of the field may be incorrigibly lazy, neither sowing nor reaping, yet the simple purple in which they are clothed outmatches the royal purple of Solomon's regalia. Such limpid illustrations enable us to see in the providence of God the pattern for human behaviour.

So Christian morality requires a pattern of behaviour to one another, which aims at the perfect copy of God's care for his creation. Jesus sets the practice of this programme within the frame of a universal family life and appeals to his hearers to remember that, within certain situations, that family relationship already exists. He was speaking to his fellow Hebrews and there existed an unparalleled tradition of such family relationships in the Hebrew story: the father who gives good gifts to his children; the family responsibility for hospitality; the killing of the fatted calf for the return of the prodigal, just because he had come home, and not because of his penitence. All these are examples of the Christian obligation to seek to meet the basic economic needs of people as a recognition of their intrinsic worth, a value which entitles them to the means of subsistence, whether they are contributors or even parasites. The basic ingredients of this moral attitude can be traced all through the troubled story of the Hebrew peoples. Jesus both purifies and enlarges its nature and scope.

He removes any trace of selectivity on the grounds of moral worth and extends its reach to cover all men, Jew and Gentile. For a Christian to quote Paul against this backcloth, that if a man will not work neither shall he eat (see 2 Thess. 3:10), assuming that to be an injunction and not a statement (as I am sure it is), should remind us that deliverances of the Apostle are of variable worth. He was about as right in matters of racism, for example, as he was often wrong about women, and he is wrong in this matter too. Here he has almost entirely misunderstood his Lord. In fact, the encouraging thing about many modern societies which make no official claim to follow Jesus, is that nevertheless they do seem to have understood him fairly well in these matters. Perhaps the most enheartening change that is taking place in some political ideologies is the growing recognition of the economic validity of the Sermon on the Mount. The Welfare State, which in varying degrees of comprehensiveness has become institutionalized in countries like Great Britain, and elements of understanding care which are being included in many modern political structures, reflect this Christian ethic in a number of its distinguishable ways. It is widely acceptable, where not so long ago it was widely ignored, that society has an obligation to keep its members alive, whether they appear able to do it for themselves or not, and must accept the initiative in the responsibility to feed the starving and to shelter the homeless. The beginnings of such a duty go back, in these islands, to the Elizabethan

Poor Law of 1601 and, in some respects, even before that. The initiative is of much more recent development.

Again, society must provide its members with the various means of life as a service to which they are entitled and which their ability to pay for is not the first requirement. If 'free' is used to designate such provisions, the word must mean, 'freely available at the point of need' and made so by the community as a whole through rates and taxes. There is no such thing as freedom in any absolute sense. Water is an example of such a free service; medical care is another and education is a third. Therefore, as an emergency instrument and as a public policy, the Welfare State is essentially Christian and we should have no hesitation in asserting that it represents a return to the ethic out of which Christianity came. Welfare has a long history, if a chequered one. The Old Testament, as I have said, is very largely an essay on the Welfare State and the moral obligation of politics to embrace it. That is why the comment, still frequently heard in our legal circles, that 'this a Court of law, not of morals', would have been unintelligible to an ancient Israelite.

What, however, must still be a Christian judgement on even the most impressive political provisions against poverty in body, mind and estate, is that so often the logical conclusions of particular practices are burked. Perhaps the most glaring illustration is in the very field where the English Poor Law began. A major point of that enactment was the poor house, the forerunner of the Victorian workhouse, whereas in matters of food, what was an emergency provision has now become a general practice. If you were thirsty you could apply for a drink of water; now you can turn the tap for it. A similar process of enlargement and availability has not unfortunately taken place as yet in other fields of human need. The provision of somewhere to live, still remains within the emergency category. Whereas health and education are service ministries today, housing is still not so, although it represents just as imperative a need as a public service in a civilized community as do the other basic human necessaries (and I use the word 'necessaries' rather than the word 'necessity', which is not nearly so accurate).

The fulfilment of the ethic declared and practised by Jesus has found a simple, yet effective, expression in circles which, officially, turn their back on religion. This should be counted for righteousness, even if the Red Star has supplanted the Cross on their cathedral spires. It was the materialistic socialism of the continent which coined the phrase 'to each according to his needs, from each according to his power'. This is the essential Gospel and the Church should not be afraid to quote it and to press it to its proper limits. Christianity declares that the genuine needs of every man are to be met around the family table and the family hearth fire. Very well, then, those who exercise political power, and especially such comprehensive power as is theirs to command, should legislate and implement legislation so that all human needs are available free of charge at the point of such needs. Thereafter the same political administration should legislate and implement legislation so that the human resources created by the satisfaction of those needs should be at the disposal of the whole society. This is the core of the political philosophy of socialism, to which I will return in a subsequent chapter. Suffice it to add, at this point, a rider on the question as to what limits should be put on the word 'need', because it is obviously not coterminous with the word 'want'. I may want a thousand pounds or a diamond brooch. I do not necessarily need the first and it is highly unlikely that I need the second. Obviously the needs covered by food, clothing and shelter are as imperative as they are unchanging.

There are however other needs which can only be a matter of practical politics when the first group have been met. When those basic needs are either assured or capable of being answered, then the area of need widens and, as it widens, includes requirements which are more mental and cultural and spiritual.

The student must be given the prolonged opportunity so to meet his intellectual needs as to render him capable of serving his fellows with a developed mind; the violinist must be given his instrument so that he can give it back in music; the ordinary people without special potential gifts must have free access to the world of beauty and culture and art so that they can civilize their environment and rescue it from a bingo squalor.

It is once again instructive to realize that one of the admirable elements in the world behind the iron or bamboo curtains, is their recognition that such needs are as fundamental as food, clothing and shelter. So many of the cultural needs, for which the capitalist world still requires payment, are a charge upon the state and available freely to its citizens. If those operating behind such curtains still fail to recognize that the spiritual need is more fundamental still, at least such folly is being increasingly seen, by many sympathetic observers, as the Achilles heel of their avowed socialism.

The adventure of giving first and receiving later does require a tremendous act of faith on the part of society, because it seems to go against the grain. Those who theoretically have been attracted by it, but who would not regard the process as ethically peremptory, are not likely to risk it, unless there is overwhelming evidence that it will work. Now the power of communism today lies not so much in the reasonableness of its propositions as in the certainty of their fulfilment. This authority is found, as the reader will know, in what is known as dialectical materialism. Now whatever else that phrase means, the all-important claim that it makes is that by a scientifically undertaken study of the past the future can be foretold without a peradventure. That future is the classless, global society in which the interminable struggles hitherto between man and his neighbour, class and class, workers and their exploiters will end once and for all. Therefore, every one of its propositions, when in line with that final purpose and carried out with that purpose in mind, must succeed, however painful, prolonged or apparently fruitless they may be in the process.

In the professedly scientific form which this theory has assumed, it must surely be rejected as untrue, because such a programme can begin only in faith, not in fact. It is in essence a faith rather than a theorem, for it presupposes a world of purpose. It believes that there is a universal truth to be dis-covered, that there is an earthly paradise to be reached and, supremely, that human beings, with all their problems and their sins, can look forward with hope. Now if that is not a religious conviction, I don't know what is! For the Christian this hope and assurance are founded on the providence of the Heavenly Father and therefore to feed the hungry is to do the will of God and so to begin to ensure the consummation of his divine purpose. Here is the practical value of the doctrine of Justification by faith. The Christian's confidence in the elimination of poverty is justified by his confidence in the love of God. Communists who have no right to it have in fact had to borrow it without acknowledgement in order to justify their own position. They are welcome to use it. One day they will see that it works because it is true.

8 Education

There can be no field of human activity where the relationships between political and Christian moral attitudes are more vividly demonstrable than in the world of education, and this for two outstanding reasons. First, governments, primitive or sophisticated, will naturally be concerned to produce a condition of acceptance, if not of co-operation, with the governed, and what more effective action can they take than to tailor the training of their subjects, particularly in their most formative years, to that end? Education will reflect the dominant ideas of the political structure where it is practised. Secondly, as was argued in an earlier chapter of this short document, the capability if not the achievement of such educational systems in producing both a brain-washed curriculum and a brain-washed scholar has almost immeasurably increased in our time. This may not be a universal truth, but it is one of the most important of all considerations, especially in this field of education. That is why it is imperative to mention it at the very beginning of any consideration of this topic.

Education has been, and still is, terrifyingly effective in some cases in conditioning those who are subject to it. For example, in the Christendom of the Middle Ages, where the attempt was made to equate

Church and State, education was predominantly ecclesiastical and was conceived as the provision of the mental equipment for those who were to be ordained, so that they could fulfil their vocations, of one sort or another, from the priest to the clerk. Education for the masses, on the other hand, was a work of charity rather than of civic duty, and the cynics have said that in many cases the Church had its own prudential reasons for education going no further. The important thing was to encourage people to make a good death rather than to equip them to live a full life. This, again, is an exaggeration, but there is a deal of truth in it. Oxford and Cambridge were religious institutions for the education in Christian behaviour of the chosen few. All the same, education was uniformly rooted in the Church, if not in the Gospel, and true learning flourished, sometimes because of the Church and sometimes in spite of it. Greek culture was often baptized or mutilated by the Church in order to fit into its own ecclesiastical dogmas and it is interesting that Islamic culture was of sterner stuff and that Christians officially made up for their inability to come to terms with its spiritual simplicities by borrowing and absorbing its mathematics.

These comments are therefore by no means exhaustive and any comprehensive view of education under Christendom would necessarily include many other considerations, but they may be sufficient to underline the truth that education reflects the philosophy of the educators. Whereas the philosophical base to which I have referred was ostensibly Christian, the base today is much more likely to be ideological and non-Christian at that.

Now what of the contemporary scene? Great Britain has opted for comprehensive education and interprets that intention in a number of specific provisions. One is to make available to all a full and uniform curriculum of teaching processes and methods and this, as I have said already, reflects the philosophy of the educators. The secular state has effectively taken over in Ankara as in London, in India and Pakistan as in Tel Aviv. The St Petersburg of yesterday almost invariably becomes the Petrograd of more recent times and in some cases, of course, the Leningrad of today. Christianity, like Islam or Buddhism, is no longer the source and instrument of educational systems, though rearguard actions are still maintained in areas of the Middle East. Political parties, such as the Christian Democrats, still include Christianity as one of their objectives and the 1944 Education Act makes the one obligatory subject in the schools within its jurisdiction 'religious instruction'. Elsewhere, the bull has been taken by the horns (to add the word 'papal' might make this a pun) and both in France and in many states across the Atlantic education is constitutionally secular. The problem therefore is in one sense simplified. Organized Christianity in these islands is no longer in a position to provide an overall educational system. It will claim the freedom to provide such educational opportunities for Christian education alongside those provided by the State. None the less, the all-important point is that education is a political achievement because progressively politics has become 'the way things happen'. The Church can criticize, commend and contribute to education but can only participate in education itself as an auxiliary voluntary body or by expressing its claim through political systems of education. Educationally, the Bishops of the Church of England can be much more effective in the House of Lords than in their own General Synod.

Maybe these general comments will be sufficient as the terms of reference in an attempt to present the Christian view on education. There is no room here for a world tour of educational systems and the Christian view of them. What is possible is to examine certain characteristics in the developing education system in Great Britain and to see where those characteristics collide or coalesce, or are capable of such modifications as to reflect a Christian morality —a Christian morality that should inform education systems everywhere.

To provide a system of Comprehensive Schools at pre-university and further education levels to take the place of—not to co-exist with—the present Secondary Modern and Grammar Schools, is to ensure in such schools all the facilities hitherto available in the curricula of the separated schools. This involves abolishing a process of selection in the eleven-plus examination, by which scholars were allocated to one or to the other educational institution, and this is done on two grounds: one, that whatever selection was desirable to fit the educational processes to the scholars' needs and capacities can be more efficiently undertaken within the comprehensive school itself and second, that the eleven-plus examination, or anything like it, was a thoroughly imperfect instrument to use for the purposes of selection in general at that age, let alone selection for separated schools. This is a rough sketch, a mandatory attitude to education expressed by one particular political authority. It is not meant to be an exhaustive treatment of what is obviously a complicated issue, but it is not an unsuitable one, as it raises certain quite fundamental questions, which are pertinent to any effort to look at education through Christian eyes and to judge educational systems in Christian terms.

Unlike questions about violence and law and order, the ethic of the Gospel as applied to education has to be largely inferential—and it is none the worse for that. It has to be read into the Gospel rather than read off from it. It begins, where all such ethical principles emerge, with the worth of the child to be educated. We believe that this child, wherever he comes from, whatever the state or assumed state of his I.Q., belongs to the Kingdom of God, and therefore is as entitled to the full requirements for the nourishment of the mind as he is entitled to adequate food, clothing and shelter for the body. This free education as a Divine Right is a true interpretation of the Gospel and it would be churlish to impugn the principle because, in practice, it is not carried

74

out to the full, as of course is the case everywhere. Where the Christian must be critical is in the substance, rather than in the concept, of this educational system. If comprehensiveness does recognize to the full the innate right to education, the expression and practice of that word in legislation does not necessarily represent fully the carrying out of that right. Here the ethic of Christianity, which the Gospel relies upon, is that of the new creature in Christ. Jesus sets a goal for human development which must go far beyond expertise and the three Rs. This new creation, new man, as Paul described him, is the whole man, in whom any separation of his mind from his body and either or both from his spirit, as if they can be treated independently of one another, is totally unacceptable. It would be difficult if not impossible to find pieces of teaching in the Gospels in which Jesus specifically prescribes the educational system which will belong to the Kingdom of God, but here St Paul has, I believe, interpreted his Master's spirit and intention.

It naturally follows that education must respect this intention and hence what is taught and the way in which it is presented as meeting that need, within a freely available framework, will determine its acceptability from a Christian standpoint: the comprehensive system, which I have briefly outlined, can serve to illustrate this. It is surely right to abolish a principle of selection, which narrows the area of education to the three Rs with the addition of some acquaintance with history and science. If selection at eleven-plus is wrong because it is practically unfair and takes place at the wrong age anyhow, it is doubly wrong in maintaining the fallacy that educational ability and attainment belong to this restricted area of human development. Instead, the comprehensive system recognizes how many human skills are capable of development and lie dormant until they are stimulated by adequate educational processes. They must be catered for in an educational system which is to nourish the whole personality of the scholar. Within the Comprehensive School, what is called 'streaming' can be accompanied by the widest range of subjects rather than the straight-jacket of a traditional uniformity. The comprehensive claim is initially justified when within such a system the individual child will have the widest opportunity of individual development, according to his particular qualities of mind or potential ability. That claim is further justifiable as the end or purpose of the Christian ethic.

A useful rider to this educational theorem is that the comprehensive system as represented in the current legislation of Great Britain is so anxious to honour this commitment that it actually makes provision outside the general scheme for special schooling for those whose later contribution to the civilized society, when they are educated, will be in the fields of music and of dancing. It may well be that comprehensive education may need to add to these provisions in the areas of further education.

One of the more interesting as well as important

changes is in fact the increase in the number of particular subjects or skills that can find a genuine place in the school curriculum. Psychology is now almost *vieux jeu* as an examination subject and the branches of scientific studies in a computer age, though not independent of one another, do demand specialized attention. The comprehensive system must not lose in depth what it achieves in breadth— the need and opportunity for specialization must not obscure the basic needs to develop judgement and intellectual responsibility. From this ethical standpoint of the mature life, as prescribed by the Gospel, there is still much to be desired and then done, if the doctrine of the whole man is to be accepted. Education is as much a preparation for citizenship as it is a possession of scholarship. And citizenship is a social art or science wherein only those who are educated to practise it will be socially literate, even if they can solve the most complicated quadratic equation or conjugate the rarest of irregular verbs. Writing of verbs, I may remind the reader that the very word *educate* comes not from the Latin word *educere*—to draw out—the latent intelligence, so to say, but from *educare*, which is to feed. The process of feeding is to nourish the entire person and such a diet must include the process of learning to relate the information that begins at the desk with the use of it which begins whenever the scholar rises from that desk. Such desk education may well end at sixteen; at any particular stage of a country's growth or a country's condition, there

77

are economic and political and social reasons for which this may be necessary. Indeed, this may be the correct age at which to cease the academic routine for scholars whose capabilities lie in areas other than what is called 'further education', and for which the Comprehensive Schools may or may not be able to provide that development, though the Technical Institute or the University may be unsuitable.

The significance of this linking of primary, secondary and further education is a logical process, and it is something more; it represents the gradual and increasing introduction into the system of the moral element. It enables the scholar first to receive the primary instruction and capacity to form correct sound judgements, and then to see that the means to a social and creative end are also there. The lack of such a practical relationship between knowledge and its usefulness is the prime cause of the alarming truancy rate among teenagers today, who see no purpose in their last years at the desk and just stay away. Here lies the present imperfection in contemporary education. Granted that the money is often not there to finance such a continued process, granted that the economic conditions of any particular time make it difficult, Christian conscience can never be satisfied with a truncated education system and must press for an absolute priority in education for a mature society. Learning in the school of life, as well as in the school at the end of the street, is no cliché unless we allow it to become one. However, lest such a sentence should smack of a typically soggy ecclesiasticism, I would suggest how in more precise terms such a claim must find expression. The clue, paradoxically enough, is to be found in countries where the dominant political characteristics were hostile to the Christian faith. The consomuls in Moscow, and the Hitler Youth in Germany years ago, possessed moral elements completely disagreeable to Christianity yet, in their insistence on National Service for youth as an element in the educational process, they had something that Christians ought to take very seriously into account. This educational system was, however, corrupted on two counts. It was directed towards a racial creed that was and always must be morally objectionable and it was geared to National Service in the armed forces. None the less, the association of book-learning with the practical responsibility of beginning to translate that learning into the real world is surely the way to make educataion, like every other human activity, sacramental. This may sound almost a presumptuous word to introduce into this argument, but there are beginnings of such a spirit in the comprehensive system. The Church must recognize this with thankfulness and hope. The response of the Church should be to encourage not to cavil, but above all to help the State education system to maintain the courage of its convictions and to press on with the proper consequences of such beginnings.

There still remains the question mentioned at the

beginning of this chapter, the association of education with political or religious ideologies, and the liberty or the lack of liberty that exists in educational systems today. What of the teachings of Marx in Soviet schools? This question and the agreed syllabus of the Education Act—the question of liberty—demands a chapter to itself. As this general issue of political and religious liberty can be vividly seen against the particular backcloth of education, I will use it as an introduction to the next chapter.

9 Liberty

Liberty offers a classic example of a word which belongs to the living world and therefore is strictly indefinable. What is meant by liberty can be experienced, that is, it can be lived through. Much of it can be described, more or less, but it cannot be defined. This does not mean that it cannot be understood and brought within the area of informed thought and certainly it is no excuse for ignoring its central position in every serious consideration of our human affairs. It may be of help to the subsequent discussion with its bearing on the politico-religious-moral question if I catalogue a few of the attempted delineations of the meaning of the word 'liberty' from the Latin and 'freedom' from the Anglo-Saxon.

'Self-determination' or 'self-determinism' are perhaps the most agreeable philosophical words; 'ordered restraint' commends itself to sociologists. I remember, with particular interest, James Ward the nineteenth-century pioneer in psychology, who opted for 'the power to obey the good'. Now these various descriptions all contain one common factor —liberty has to do with the elimination of various restraints and a description of the particular form that any restraints that remain must take. In a word, liberty cannot be the absence of restraint, or the removal of any impediment to wilful action, for no such absolute condition is possible. This platitude, however, is an imperative text with which to introduce the topic here. All the other attributes of liberty depend on this initial proposition: freedom is invariably conditional. All the same, it must mean the negation of arbitrary and largely external restrictions upon human beings and upon human behaviour preventing the achievement of desired ends. What prohibitions, controls and restrictions on human activity are acceptable or unacceptable depends on the worthwhileness of those desired ends and political and religious judgements on such ends. To give this abstract consideration of liberty a local habitation and a name, the problems that it raises in the world of education will serve and can be usefully set out in a number of questions from that field.

Can children or their parents in a comprehensive system, for example, be free to choose the sort of education they want? Are either the compulsory subject of Religious Instruction geared to Christian foundations or ideological instruction based on Marxist foundations consistent with freedom? To what extent is liberty in educational processes compatible with authority, as between scholar and teacher? It must be clear, straight away, that education is in itself a progress from the lack of personal freedom which ignorance imposes, to the exercise of personal freedom that knowledge bestows, and therefore at the initial stage choice has to be made by others than the scholar himself. That is, once again, a platitude, but it is an important correction of the idea of unrestricted liberty, as some people are advocating it today, even within Primary Schools. The freedom which is at the end depends on the discipline at the beginning.

To a degree the same is true of parents; they should not try to prescribe for their children when they are not free to judge their genuine requirements, though to take away from them this parental authority or power of guidance would be quite wrong. Here is one of the delicate balances which still, in any civilized system, has to be measured and accepted. Freedom is indeed ordered restraint, and in so many aspects the community as a whole is better equipped than even the most concerned of parents to order the kind of restraint which will finally liberate and not restrict the scholar. Now there is nothing to turn to in the ethics of the Christian Gospel, there is nothing in the teaching of Jesus, which advocates a liberty in any sphere which is not in itself the fruit of discipline, a discipline which has to accept at some stage and in some degree an outside authority. The emphasis of Jesus on the role of the servant is succinctly expressed in the phrase from the hymn 'Firmly bound, for ever free'. In education, then, as in every other realm, there must be a place for authority as a prerequisite of liberty. Further, the more widespread and comprehensive authority becomes in the interests of freedom generally, the more that authority must not fall unevenly and discriminately on individuals.

Here again, our old acquaintance 'compromise' rears its head. An example can, once again, be taken from the field of education. In an officially Christian country, the public authority will naturally enough consider that the educational system should reflect, or give prominence to, declared Christian ideas. This will always mean a certain disadvantage or reduction of opportunity to a non-Christian scholar; in an increasingly secular and multi-racial society one scholar's freedom to receive Christian teaching or instruction becomes another scholar's deprivation of similar teaching or instruction in the Jewish or the Moslem faith, to which he may belong, unless time be found in the curriculum for the instruction of an ever-increasing number of faiths, and this is practically quite impossible. Therefore there is no one hundred per cent solution to the problem of one person's freedom, which is so often someone else's disadvantage. Only an approximate answer, and a compromise one at that, is on the cards. The least unsatisfactory way of resolving the dilemma is the democratic one. The majority view should prevail; the minority will thereby experience a loss of liberty, but that minority must never be regarded as having lost its rights because it was not numerous enough.

This is the perennial problem and once again the field of education provides a suitable example.

Education in the Soviet Union is indoctrination, so it is in China and so it was in Christendom, as we have seen. In the process of indoctrination or, if indoctrination is too strong a word, the incalculation of prescribed ideas, Marxism is not only a specific school subject, it is the point of departure and the cherished and declared destination of all subjects. The little red book is to the Chinese youth today what the Bible was to the medieval scholar. It should be added that not only battles were won on the playing fields of Eton, the victories of Capitalism and Imperialism and Colonialism were achieved there as well. Now this is intolerable in the light of Christian ethics. You cannot love God with your mind if that mind is kept bare of every piece of intellectual furniture except that which is acceptable or desirable in order to accommodate your life to the prevailing situation. Something of this has already been treated in the last chapter. You cannot seek the Kingdom of God if its whereabouts and condition cannot even be examined; you cannot make a free judgement about truth if you are denied the opportunity even to get to know what it is you are told to disagree with, and the Christian tradition must, over and over again, come under that kind of indictment.

Liberty is always dependent on the social restraint of society and the kind of restraint employed will be governed by the nature of that society. I will in the next chapter try to outline the sort of society wherein there is a maximum of personal liberty within a framework of responsible public authority. The rest of this chapter will contain some comments offerd in respect of the foregoing considerations of the problems associated with liberty in the field of economics, political power and personal behaviour. These considerations will, I hope, show that there is a necessary place for that authority in the achievement or protection of freedom; that majority rule is unavoidable, even if it considerably impairs the freedom of the minority; that temporary compromises are unavoidable because circumstances put limits to what is physically possible. Christian ethics must accept this. There is no alternative in common sense to the recognition of these regulations and restrictions.

It is in the form it assumes in the light of these considerations that the morality of the Gospel is involved. How does the use of economic power, or political power effect personal freedom and to what extent should this happen? Economically, the new-found power of organized labour in the trade union movement and expressed in strike action, is both an expression of the struggle for liberty by those hitherto the victims of a class system, and the denial of liberty to large numbers of their fellow workers as well as their employers in the community at large. This represents a recent and enormously important change in social power. Political power exercised by parliaments, political classes, regimes of various hues from personal to radical, through oligarchies and monarchies to fascisms and brands of com-

munism and dictatorship, all these are all too
familiar in the amount of freedom that they sever-
ally permitted or encouraged or abolished. This
exercise of political power is justifiable or not to the
Christan conscience in so far as it is the ordered
restraint necessary to free the ordinary citizen to
develop his own ability to pursue the good life.
There can be no doubt whatsoever that, in most of
the cases hinted at in this last paragraph, this restriction of freedom is unjustifiable and there is
ample evidence that the end product is not the free
man but, in so many cases, the conditioned man;
the man ready to accept outside directions rather
than to rely upon his own individual capacity, within a framework of ordered restraint, to add to the
wealth of the community in which he lives.

Democracy—that is, the prevailing will of the
majority freely expressed—is, as I have tried to
argue, the only ready, if rough, method of assessing
and putting that power into effect. What is new is
the emergence of economic power which can prove
as decisive as the powers hitherto within the competence of governments. The liberty of the subject
can no longer be altogether safeguarded by political
acts at Westminster. Economic acts at Smith Square
may checkmate any legislative act by paralyzing the
community with strike action. This is a bleak truth,
but it is an incontestable one. So long as labour was
largely unorganized, it was powerless to challenge
its economic masters and insignificant in comparison
with Parliamentary authority. Now, only a social

contract between the citizen in the trade unions and the citizen in the House of Commons will meet this new and revolutionized situation. In this unprecedented development, the Church must develop an industrial philosophy, as once the nonconformist conscience expressed the philosophy of political freedom in nineteenth-century liberalism, and the Christian Socialists and the I.L.P. campaigned for the dignity of the individual within the Parliamentary systems of their day.

Here however is a problem. The Christian ethic that demands immediate attention must insist that the new wine of corporate economic power is put into a new sort of social barrel. This is its prime task but, in the meantime, it is the business of the Church to distinguish, if it can, between the legitimate and illegitimate use of strike action. On the one hand, there is the refusal of workers to co-operate in an industrial process in which they believe that injustice is being done; on the other, there is the strike which is a form of violence which treats the community as a pawn in a sectional game. The distinction is fundamental, though particular expressions of these two kinds of industrial behaviour may be highly complicated. The Church must also surely insist that work with a high content of vocation, such as nursing, or work that is absolutely necessary for the public safety and welfare, such as the police force, carries with it an obligation which prohibits general strike action. In areas like these, it would be impudent to pretend that the Church can at present make any final pronouncement, even if it were desperately minded to do so. Like M.P.s and Trade Union leaders, the Church is faced with a new social phenomenon—the emergence of co-ordinated economic power, and churchmen must learn before they can teach. The foregoing in this chapter can at least provide a stimulus to such a process of education.

However, a chapter on liberty would be unpardonably incomplete if it omitted reference to the more personal activities of human beings as they are, or ought to be, affected by political action. How far is a State justified in seeking to control the use of tobacco or of various sexual acts performed in private? It there any Christian justification for the invasion of privacy in what a man wears, if he is wearing it on a motor cycle? Now the last of these particular questions or illustrations can indicate an answer that meets the case behind all of them. Christianity must insist that heaven and hell are moral realities in whatever form they assume, only if men and women are free to make their own way to one or the other. In the last analysis, personal responsibility is all, and religion is what a man does with his loneliness. That loneliness is his right. To the extent therefore that smoking, or homosexual acts in private, and wearing turbans are within that sphere of loneliness, men and women should be at liberty from any external law and left to the prophets. The moment, however, a Sikh wearing his turban takes to the road on a lethal machine like a motor bicycle, he begins to involve others; he emerges from that loneliness. It could be argued that he should not by law be punished for committing suicide on the road (or of course botching the job) but inasmuch as a road accident may well cause injuries to others besides the particular motor-cyclist, what he puts on his head ceases to be a private matter and becomes a public issue. In addition to the widespread injury to others, an accident under such conditions will certainly impose burdens on public authorities like the police, medical services and the treasury.

The same is true of the habit of smoking, which predisposes the smoker to cancer, and therefore its effects widen out not only into the society of his family but engage more and more of the time and medical resources of the whole community.

In the case of sexual practices of various kinds, even those who champion the permissive society, which would identify most sexual acts as belonging to the personal realm, must surely recognize that, whatever may be their moral attitude to the performance of such acts, one man's sexual freedom becomes another man or woman's sexual slavery, and if they are still in doubt let them consult any probation officer or social worker anywhere. We do not live in two worlds; one in which social invasion of personal behaviour is required as the guardian of liberty and the other in which that social invasion is unjustified because we are free to do what we like with our own lives and it is nobody else's business. In practical terms, the difference where it exists is one of degree not of kind. The ethical standpoint of Christianity is that the rightness or wrongness of political actions which curtail individual freedom is determined by the social involvement, and the degree of that involvement must regulate the stringency of those political restraints.

Liquor control, restrictions on its sale, the sale and licensing laws themselves, are not justified because alcohol is the 'devil in solution', as some teetotallers seem to imagine. Both total abstinence and government intrusion into what is personally imbibed is necessary because a private intake of intoxicating liquor is inseparable from effects that may well add up to a social calamity. The restriction demanded in this field, as with drugs and driving, ought to be increased since the dangers of social consequences unquestionably have increased. On the other hand, the savage penal restrictions on homosexual and other deviant sexual practices need to be considered more compassionately by the Church. Many of them may be morally innocuous in themselves. I cannot see anything wrong when two adult homosexuals give some physical expression to their love for one another. The traditional distaste for homosexuality by the so-called normal majority, backed up if not fermented by ecclesiastical misrepresentation of sex itself, is no excuse for ferocious laws which have little, if anything, to do with social security. This is no plea for moral indifference, but it is a plea for genuine personal freedom, and Christian ethics has the difficult task of holding the true balance so that liberty does not degenerate into licence and, at the same time, public responsibility does not usurp that freedom.

The reader will not have failed to notice how contingent most of this chapter, in substance, has been. This, as in the previous question of education, is due to the imperfections of the author fully to describe the topic in which he has invited the attention of the reader, but it is due as well to his inability to marry the claims of individual freedom and of corporate restraint in a society which, I have repeatedly argued, renders such a marriage impossible or offers little hope that it will be fruitful. The next and final chapter will therefore attempt to indicate what, in economic and political terms, that society should look like, for to give some recognizable picture of the structure of such a society is indispensable if the practical demands that the present society so obviously and critically presents are to be seen against the backcloth of what churchmen call the Kingdom of God. Such a society may at one and the same time meet those practical demands and provide the environment of that Kingdom.

10 Socialism

So, finally, is there an economic and political form in which the Gospel can be expressed? The contention of these pages is that there must be, if Christianity is to be offered as a way of life here as well as preparation for life hereafter. A further contention is that the Gospel does in fact provide such a form. It says what the Kingdom of God means in time. Well, if that is so, then in consequence, as the argument of the last chapter concludes, those who advocate these claims must not avoid the responsibility of saying what that form Christianity must take, really is. The tactical demand for such a translation of the Gospel is as overwhelming in the light of economic and political significance today as the theological demand has been intrinsic from the moment Pilate set the inscription. 'This is Jesus the King of the Jews' over the Cross on which Jesus died. A relevant Gospel today must contain very much more, one might well say infinitely more, than political means; it cannot contain less.

I hope that enough has been said already to justify the contention that much of the ethic of that Gospel has of necessity only been applicable, piecemeal, in the 'bread and butter' side of life. The failure to universalize the Gospel is due to the historic fact that up till now there has not been an overall economic framework either which fully incorporated its message or made possible the fulfilment of its claims. The ethical teaching of Jesus, where it has been taken seriously, in societies calling themselves Christian, has at best been an approximation and a compromise, and one element in this state of human affairs has been that for the completion of the enterprise the appropriate tools and ingredients were either inadequate or were not then available. You can make a purse out of a sow's ear, what you cannot do is make a *silk* purse.

Unfortunately, what has happened all too often in the Church's story has been that either through a preoccupation with makeshift purses, or through the not unnatural conclusion, as the Kingdom tarries, that there isn't enough silk around anyway, the considered structure of that ideal society has either been ignored or indefinitely postponed. By all means at their command Christians in society are called upon to make the best of a bad job, but this is no fulfilment of the law or the prophets. They have to hold the mirror up to the nature of the society which will indeed give outline and substance to the Kingdom of God. The true Church is both the workshop of the Kingdom for today and the offer of the blueprint of the Kingdom for tomorrow.

So to the answer to this question in both thought and action — I believe that socialism is the expression of that part of the Christian ethic which properly has to do with politics and economics, and any meaningful consideration of such a claim absolutely requires, as I invited the reader in the opening pages of this document to agree, that we come to some arrangement as to what the word 'socialism' means. The history of the word goes back at least as far as Homer. There was a character named Thersites who called himself a socialist, and the word has been used to describe varying degrees of public control over private behaviour, in all kinds of societies through the centuries. I suggest that 'socialism', in any precise and finished meaning, can be subsumed under a few theoretical heads.

In economic terms, it means the common ownership of the means of production, distribution and exchange, of those commodities and services which are of prime concern for the life of a human society. This does not mean the abolition of private property, and no one wants to socialize false teeth. What it does mean is that none can claim private possession of something which is socially required, if and when such possession will give to the possessor a measure of power or undue influence over his neighbour. It does need emphasis in some quarters that socialism is not the absence of wealth but of the naked power that wealth exercises in the capitalist systems. Money is a not unsuitable means of conducting exchange. When, however, it becomes in itself the means of authority, let alone exploitation, its usefulness ends and abuse takes over.

The so-called continental socialist would derive the requirement or inevitability of socialism from the scientific examination of the problems of living together in society as a whole. The Christian socialist would see it as a natural consequence of the message of the Sermon on the Mount and the example of the primitive Church.

Socialism is equally concerned, in the second place, with the proper ends of such production, distribution and exchange. It asserts the right of everybody to possess the means of life and lays upon society as a whole the duty to safeguard that right as its priority. Here, the emphasis of the family concept, as I have stressed in an earlier chapter, is more central among the Christian socialists than among those who stay more closely to a materialistic approach. The two propositions just stated are primarily economic. The political as distinguishable from the economic principle in socialism is an extension both of democratic government and equality before the law, but it has a clear-cut purpose in that extension, which is not necessarily expressed by either of them. Socialism is a classless, raceless and, in the exact sense of the word, stateless condition. Socialism may have to begin in one country, and experiments in this country, in Sweden and in Australia can be called as evidence in this respect. There is abundant evidence of true elements of socialism taking root in erstwhile capitalist states all over the world today, and our own island story should be included in any comprehensive discussion of this part of the socialist programme and activity. Socialism can begin among people of one colour—Sweden again is an example; it can also take root in one class and, without accepting the doctrine of

96

the dictatorship of the proletariat, it is surely reasonable to think that the great majority of the working class can be such a vanguard in the socialist campaign.

Essentially, however, socialism is the assertion of one world-wide human family, living under one roof, enjoying a world government which will be made possible by the elimination of the injustices and provocations of violences which exist in other forms of human association. This universality is common to both strands of socialist thought; though, as I have indicated, why materialists who deny ultimate purpose to life can find it possible to embrace such a principle poses a real problem for the philosophy of politics. I am concerned here with the immediate question as to whether this social ideology and programme is in fact a corollary of Christian principles. Calling as evidence in support of socialism the teaching of Jesus requires a closer look at the New Testament and at the record of his life and teaching than some social gospellers have given it.

Jesus knew nothing of the ramifications of a complex industrialized society. He only had time to lay down the first principles of human community. Crucified at thirty, he had no time to monitor the practical effects of his own teaching, as his faithful followers began to practise it. Moreover, what we know of that teaching comes to us through the limited understanding of men and women who only partially appreciated its breadth and its sweep. Above all, the limits of the Roman occupation imposed what were tantamount to impossibilities in the carrying out of

97

that message, and this Roman *imperium* persuaded many of the disciples of Jesus that his Kingdom could only come by divine and dramatic intervention from on high, and caused them to regard the Gospel for society as a strictly interim measure while the Apocalypse was awaited. What is so tremendous in the light of these comments, is the corpus of teaching that *has* been preserved and its conquest, as it were, of the limitations that might have appeared insuperable. The fact is that imperfect though the record is, the true significance of this teaching has been preserved. It is, if you like, a miracle. It is certainly of supreme importance for the Christian of today. The Gospel is not a personal announcement with a number of social matters appended to it; it is personal because it is at heart social. The family setting is omnipresent and the Lord's Prayer has only to be listened to in order to justify the claim that the common responsibility of the family for the welfare of its members is a perfect foundation from which to build the argument for Clause 4, the article in the creed of the Labour Party which asserts the common ownership referred to above.

The family ethic which authorizes public welfare as of right has already been considered and it is not only explicit in the Sermon on the Mount but has its sublime vindication in the Cross, on which its spokesmen died. 'God so loved the world that he gave his only Son' is the supreme example of giving as the essential activity of love. As God gives, so must we, and not of calculation but of faith in its rightness and its effectiveness. It was Heine—the German poet—who said that he too would have been prepared to give his life for others had he not shrewdly suspected that they weren't worth it. In absolute contradiction is the Christian conviction that while we were yet sinners Christ gave himself for us. For the obvious reason that the killing of Jesus took place after three years, at most, in which his teaching could have taken root, it is not surprising that there is little in the Gospels of the detailed political and social form that such teaching was to produce, and the reason for this dearth of precise teaching is obvious. The mission and the public ministry of Jesus were contingent and he knew that what he advocated was little better than good advice in theory, without the power to carry it out. That power he vouchsafed to all who believe in him, when he died for us. Nothing is so clear in the Gospels as the certainty in the mind of Jesus that such power to turn good advice into good news could only be released in the creative suffering of the servant of the Kingdom. To me this is the superlative insight. It is the power of non-violent love to accomplish the will of God through suffering, and to open up the Kingdom of Heaven to all believers. The Cross is the Gospel of the teaching. Therefore the final justification of socialism, as Christianity in practice, can only be found 'Anno Domini' and sure enough there it is in the Acts of the Apostles. They found the ability to carry out the teaching of their Master in the power of his Cross. There, in the second and in the fourth chapters, is socialism in practice. Common ownership, the family table, the family hearth, the family responsibility and, in the case of Ananias and Sapphira, its sanctity and the mortal crime of betraying it.

This Apostolic socialism—or communism, if you prefer the word, with a small 'c'—was of comparatively short duration, though its example has been followed time and time again in communes, kibbutzim and religious orders down the centuries. The story of the Church's growing relationships with the Roman Empire has been somewhat cynically told in the following terms: that both sides preferred to practise the dubious advice 'if you can't beat 'em, join 'em'. This may be altogether too harsh a judgement but it is a matter of fact that official Christianity abandoned common ownership in favour of the rights of private property, instituted a class distinction as between clergy and laity, and increasingly identified itself with the Northern hemisphere and the Mediterranean culture. As a warning of the way in which sinful men corrupt the highest example set by saintly men, such a declension could be regarded as one among many instances of the awesome power of evil. What makes the story more deplorable in this particular context is that main-line Christianity has justified this abandonment of apostolic practice as being in error, and has invested the alternatives to it with a theological justification to which they are not entitled.

Let us look at this ecclesiastical process more closely. Christians are called upon to believe in the gift of the Holy Spirit to guide them into all the truth. There can be no theological doubt about this primary commitment. Those first apostles who had been made aware of the Christian message and of the Lord's resurrection and ascension were bidden to await the Holy Spirit's energies which, when bestowed upon them, would baptize them with the power to do the things which their Lord had commanded and to triumph in the doing of them. The day of Pentecost duly came; they were so baptized; the Christian Church was born and the Kingdom was taken in hand. For the Church subsequently to say that this apostolic adventure in a socialist community was a mistake and that the Church had officially to correct this mistake must surely present a profound theological difficulty. If the first thing that the Apostle did after receiving the Holy Spirit's guidance and power was to make a mistake, then is not the validity of the doctrine itself completely undermined and the Church itself, to that extent, discredited? I prefer to believe that it was the Church that made the mistake and organized Christianity has suffered from this grievous error ever since. I am aware that many ideas and practices have acquired the socialist label. The contention here is that, in the terms described, socialism is not only compatible with the Christian Gospel, but is its true expression in political terms.

However, such an expression of the Gospel in a political creed can only come alive when it is corporated in an institutional frame. Looking at it from another angle, actual politics is party politics. This is a general rule to which there are very few exceptions. A consensus in political proceedings on specific issues

101

or occasional coalition governments in emergency situations like war might be cited as such exceptions, but they only serve to prove the rule, and the professed hostility to party politics, as if it is a degradation of genuine political action, should be treated with caution; in fact, it should be rejected. For example, the cry so often heard 'keep party politics out of local government' often means in fact 'keep left-wing party politics out of local government'. Apart from absolute monarchies and totalitarian dictatorships, which may or may not make use of political parties—and the more sophisticated they were, as in Franco's Spain, the more likely they were to depend on some kind of party backing—parties are for practical purposes the required instruments of political action. Hence a judgement, from Christian standards, of parties and a practical attitude to them is directly implied, and the avoidance of either or both of these implications must be repudiated. There is, I hope, no need to state again the indictment of a so-called Christian ethic which is solely applied to private piety. This is as impossible to carry out as it is to conceive.

There remains another reason or excuse for non-participation in party politics and it looks more plausible, but I am sure that it is equally wrong. It is rooted in the undeniable fact that parties of all shades of political opinion are imperfect instruments. Proceeding upon this undeniable fact, Christians who dislike compromise tend to withhold their political support from all party affairs because there is no one party with which they can wholeheartedly and whole-mindedly agree.

Now there may be occasions, such as prevailed in Hitler's Germany, when loyalty to Jesus Christ meant separation from every political body that was then extant, but generally the compromise has to be accepted. In principle, this is so for reasons which have been all too obvious in recent times. To withdraw from party politics because no party completely attracts your confidence or expresses your own convictions, opens the door to dictatorship. Tyrants come to power and flourish on the backs of those who opt out of political activity, even more than from the efforts of their own supporters, or indeed the rectitude or the credibility of their own arguments. The philosophy of Nazism is an example of the fatuous nature of its creed, but it is also evidence of its extreme effectiveness as the ideological buttress of this disgraceful regime, and it was made possible by the political abstention on the part of liberal and democratic-minded Germans. Part of the actual vigilance required to preserve freedom is the choice, however difficult, which has to be made between a number of political parties, none of which is perfect, but one of which may be sufficiently, or must be regarded as sufficiently, preferable, in most of its main intentions at least, to the others and therefore *faute de mieux* is entitled to the citizen's support. Now let me spell that out a little more carefully and then seek to apply it in some detail.

A citizen of this country who is also a citizen, by

the grace of God, of the Kingdom of Heaven on earth, will have to come to terms with the political situation in which he finds himself. One item among those terms is a choice between existing political parties as they are at the time when he is able to exercise his franchise. That choice must accept the limiting factor that none of them can give complete satisfaction and so the citizen has no option but to compare their respective merits or demerits by a yardstick which does not simply measure right from wrong. He has no such absolute choice at any polling station; what he must do is to ask himself two related questions, then act on the answers he finds to them. First, does a particular party represent an ideology, a programme, which in itself is contrary to the Christian ethic? If the answer is yes, then that is a thoroughgoing reason for not supporting it. If the answer is no, then the second question comes into play: does that party which in theory is consistent with the Christian interpretation contain within itself the practical possibilities of moving progressively nearer to its application and to the goal of that purpose? These questions are pragmatic in intention and, though the honest answer to them will so often be marginal as well as complicated, the citizen cannot leave these questions in suspense. The will must decide the deed, so as an appendix I will venture an exercise in such inexorable political choice.

We will start with Toryism. Toryism is a political theorem expressed economically in capitalism and politically in conservatism. Dependent, as it is, on the operation of enlightened self-interest, which is its own definition, it has never needed a philosophy of politics to sustain it. It has relied upon the mutual effectiveness of giving as free rein as possible to the personal incentives of gain and advancement, believing that the interplay of such basic human characteristics will blunt or even cancel out any evil effects of such selfishness and, to be fair to the Tories, will produce effects which contribute to the common good. This is the ideological framework, but within it have been drawn all sorts of economic and political pictures. The blending of individual enterprise and incentive with a technological capacity in this modern world, have undoubtedly produced the most tremendous achievements in the world of production. Alongside this development, modern Toryism has been compelled to borrow from other ideologies in order to secure some better distribution of those achievements. It would be churlish not to accept the facts that many Tory programmes are, in fact, much better than Tory philosophy. Nevertheless, on the basis of the first question, a Christian has to ask himself whether or not a party which represents the dogma of enlightened self-interest, which is after all selfishness illegally baptized, whatever its achievements or modifications, is at root contrary to the gospel of unselfish love and mutual care. Honest politicians of the Right recognize this and, as has already been pointed out, have abandoned the Christian ethic and set up another in its place. Has the reader ever heard for instance of a Christian Tory movement? There is certainly a Christian Socialist movement. Are not the words 'Christian Tory' essentially contradictory? I believe so, and therefore without aspersion on the personnel of the Conservative Party, at any particular time, an aspersion which would be morally insufferable, I am satisfied that on doctrinal grounds it cannot be supported and so the second question does not arise.

Whatever the behaviour patterns of the Tory, Christian ethics and Tory ethics are as different as chalk is from cheese. The issue of Liberalism in the Liberal Party is markedly different. The concept of liberty and, at the beginning of the century, the non-conformist conscience, embraced in the Liberal move-ment two ethical ideas which, at bottom, had a great deal to do with the Christian view of society. Liberal parties have sponsored, and continue to sponsor, pro-jects which are ethically quite the antithesis of Toryism. They are contemporary efforts to widen public control, to secure participation in industry, to oppose all forms of arbitrary power, to secure truly proportional representation in Parliament as well as in industry, and these are by no means anti-pathetic to Christian ethics. Therefore, where the only choice available to a Christian elector is between a Liberal Party and a Tory Party, then particularly on the basis of the answer to the second question, Liberalism would be preferable.

The emergence, however, of the Labour parties, and of course of Communist parties of various kinds, widens that choice and alters the situation for the elector. It brings him back once again to the first question. The parties of the Left are not only practically opposed to Toryism, they stand for ideologies which totally reject its main thesis. Liberalism does not. It is not ideological as they are, and I would not be unfair to the Liberal Party. Historically its moral fervour, its persistent efforts to remove social evils, its enthusiasm for the future, must be recognized and acclaimed without any trace of condescension. But it has never asked the fundamental question that Socialism poses: Is society sound at heart and therefore a suitable area for evolutionary improvement, or is it sick at heart and therefore in need of revolutionary change? Socialism does ask such a question and asserts the need for a new society, not an improved edition of the existing one. So where a party of the Left does offer a foundation for economic and political action which opposes Toryism with an entirely different world view, it fills a gap which Liberalism has been unable to bridge. Consequently, and other things being equal, the Christian must support a revolutionary party with a policy of politics to justify it, rather than one which leaves this basic consideration largely out of account. I write 'other things being equal': that is the compatibility of the revolutionary purpose of that party with Christian principles, and this is critical. It is surely impossible for one who interprets these principles in pacifist and democratic ways to identify himself with orthodox Marxists, if any still exist. He can admire and support elements in Communist programmes, which are far more Christian than some elements in capitalist ones, but there are inbuilt elements in Communism which, at best, are heresies of Christian thinking and, at worst, reproduce some of the most objectionable examples of Capitalist class government.

So to the Labour Party. Let us agree that it began in these islands as a movement of protest against the injustices practised upon working people and as a party specifically concerned to champion their rights. To that extent it was an intensification of Liberalism, but from its earliest Parliamentary days it contained within its ranks, and particularly within the ranks of the Independent Labour Party which was one of its foundation members, socialists who were determined to make the Labour Party the vehicle of a revolutionary movement, and to see that such a socialist community was democratically achieved. In its professed intentions and ambitions it became socialist, though it was ready to welcome into its ranks Social Democrats, Social Reformers and from right, left and centre, enthusiasts for economic change, who could be broadly regarded as revolutionary themselves. That is still the Labour Party today, with all the added dimension of office and the added difficulties of doing in government what it advocated in opposition. This is no place to argue about the justifiable compromise of a mixed economy or the ability of the Labour Party here or anywhere else to keep in double harness those who still think of it as a party for the working class of a particular country or a vehicle for the advancement of purely Trades Union projects and those who envisage for it a much more comprehensive role. The real question is—can it become the agent of the Socialism that I have argued for and insisted upon as the economic and political form that Christianity ought to demand? I would answer that, in promise more than in performance, this is possible. There is nothing inherent in the Labour Party, as there is in the Tory Party, to inhibit such a process and it is the business of the Church to facilitate and encourage that process, with constructive criticism no doubt, but with overall approval. Herein lies the clue to the answer to that second question to which so many today are inclined to give a dusty answer: does the party which is capable, in theory, of achieving Christian ends stand, in the world of politics, a practical chance of succeeding?

To say that this is the basis of a widespread cynicism as to the viability of Socialism here and elsewhere and more particularly of a particular Labour Party to achieve it, is an understatement, but it is a lifeless comment as it stands. To ask what other factors in the contemporary scene account for the cynicism is much more worth while, and it is a question to which there is, I think, a very comprehensive and satisfactory answer.

There is beyond doubt a cultivated propaganda that socialism, far from being the hope of the future, is the curse of the present. Highly irrelevant claims in this field are based on State Capitalist regimes like the U.S.S.R. and China, as if they were examples of true socialism, which they most certainly are not. In any case, such propaganda is entirely premature. We do not know yet what a socialist community will be like. All that has come to hand is what happens in places like Sweden or indeed in this country, where large elements of socialism have been mingled with other elements, which are certainly not socialist at all. Socialism, like Christianity, has not been tried and found wanting. It has been found difficult and not tried, or not tried sufficiently comprehensively for the correct deductions to be made from that effort. Behind the effectiveness of this sort of cynical propaganda lies a factor which is epidemic at present; it is faithlessness. For some it is the abandonment of a faith once held and no longer supportable, but I would imagine that, for a far greater number, it is a condition which is not the result of a change from belief to unbelief. It is an attitude and outlook, which they have breathed in from their environment, and in that environment the prevailing climate has been a faithless one. Not only in matters of religion is this so. There are of course fewer Christians about who still sing with assurance 'These things shall be: a loftier race than e'er the world hath known shall rise'; there are fewer Communists, to my knowledge, who hail the dawning of the classless society as a foregone conclusion. There is a general climate of agnosticism, a miasma of faithlessness. There are fewer members of the Labour Movement who sing the 'Red Flag', not only because they know the words (and that's quite a rare achievement), but because it beckons them to the classless society that is to be. This decline of faith and its elder brother hope, are the governing factors, both in the explanation of political and religious failures up to date but, more especially, in the prospects for tomorrow. It is not an extravagance to say that only those who are convinced that what is morally right can never be politically wrong can summon up the required enthusiasm and effort for a worthwhile future. It is only such an ultimate conviction that can withstand the assaults of the world, the flesh and the devil, especially when such assaults seem to be so successful. It is hard indeed to work for God or for the classless society or indeed for the Labour Party—and to keep going, let alone be cheerful. To proclaim peace in the nuclear age, justice in a divided world and social tranquillity in multi-racial societies is a herculean task, even for the strongest believer in such an earthly paradise.

Will socialism work? Or more particularly will it work through partial, compromised political parties and in the hands of frail and unsatisfactory human beings such as we have been and, for all the ministrations of the Christian religion, still are? The speculative answer must be that nobody knows; that the auguries are certainly not promising, and if the record of the past were the only inscription over the prospects of the Labour Party for the future, then I am afraid it fails to meet the second requirement of a viable political instrument.

However, as runs through all that is written here, if we first have good news about the future, then it is possible to take good advice for today. The infusion of hope and faith into a programme which rests upon

that goodness is the practical answer to this question:
what is morally right cannot be politically wrong.
That is the driving force that can make a programme,
however difficult, begin to work, but only if that
morality is part of the stuff with which creation is
held together. The great religious tradition from
Judaism to Christianity, through Islam, indeed Communism, holds this in substance to be true. Christians
would claim that such a confidence finds its perfect
expression in the second stage in that sequence and
that Islam emasculates some of the roots of Christian
moral truths just as Communism distorts others, but
they are all one in a world-embracing faith and in
the final victory of truth and goodness. This small
book is dedicated to that proposition. It argues that
such a consummation requires a political and
economic commitment—more extensive, more complicated than ever before but, first and foremost, it
insists that such an end must first be enlivened by
hope and then energized by faith on the part of those
who pursue it, if they are to continue to the end and
not to faint by the way. This is the very water of life.
There is no substitute for theology. The brotherhood
of man is an idle dream until and unless we first can
be assured of the Fatherhood of God. But once that
hope and faith in God, the Heavenly Father, begins
to garrison the minds and hearts of the would-be
brothers on this earth, then all things are possible to
him who believes. And if indeed this sounds like the
end of a sermon, let economists and politicians and
parsons and people, say 'Amen'.